BUILDING A CAREER IN CYBERSECURITY

BUILDING A CAREER IN CYBERSECURITY

The Strategy and Skills
You Need to Succeed

YURI DIOGENES

✦✦ Addison-Wesley

Boston • Columbus • New York • San Francisco • Amsterdam • Cape Town
Dubai • London • Madrid • Milan • Munich • Paris • Montreal • Toronto • Delhi
Mexico City • São Paulo • Sydney • Hong Kong • Seoul • Singapore • Taipei • Tokyo

For information about buying this title in bulk quantities, or for
special sales opportunities (which may include electronic versions;
custom cover designs; and content particular to your business, training goals, marketing focus, or branding interests), please contact our
corporate sales department at corpsales@pearsoned.com or (800)
382-3419.

For government sales inquiries, please contact
governmentsales@pearsoned.com.

For questions about sales outside the U.S., please contact
intlcs@pearson.com.

Visit us on the Web: informit.com/aw

Library of Congress Control Number: 2023939921

Copyright © 2024 Pearson Education, Inc.

Cover image: M-vector/Shutterstock

ISBN-13: 978-0-13-821451-7
ISBN-10: 0-13-821451-4

2 2023

Editor-in-Chief
Mark Taub

Executive Editor
Loretta Yates

Associate Editor
Shourav Bose

Development Editor
Rick Kughen

Project Editor
Mary Roth

Copy Editor
Rick Kughen

Indexer
Timothy Wright

Proofreader
Barbara Mack

Technical Reviewer
Nicholas DiCola

Cover Designer
Chuti Prasertsith

Figure Credits

Pearson's Commitment to Diversity, Equity, and Inclusion

Pearson is dedicated to creating bias-free content that reflects the diversity of all learners. We embrace the many dimensions of diversity, including but not limited to race, ethnicity, gender, socioeconomic status, ability, age, sexual orientation, and religious or political beliefs.

Education is a powerful force for equity and change in our world. It has the potential to deliver opportunities that improve lives and enable economic mobility. As we work with authors to create content for every product and service, we acknowledge our responsibility to demonstrate inclusivity and incorporate diverse scholarship so that everyone can achieve their potential through learning. As the world's leading learning company, we have a duty to help drive change and live up to our purpose to help more people create a better life for themselves and to create a better world.

Our ambition is to purposefully contribute to a world where:

- Everyone has an equitable and lifelong opportunity to succeed through learning.

- Our educational products and services are inclusive and represent the rich diversity of learners.

- Our educational content accurately reflects the histories and experiences of the learners we serve.

- Our educational content prompts deeper discussions with learners and motivates them to expand their own learning (and worldview).

While we work hard to present unbiased content, we want to hear from you about any concerns or needs with this Pearson product so that we can investigate and address them.

- Please contact us with concerns about any potential bias at https://www.pearson.com/report-bias.html.

Dedication

I dedicate this book to all my students that are always asking me questions with the intent to learn more about cybersecurity and be a better professional.

CONTENTS AT A GLANCE

Foreword..xiv

Introduction...xv

Acknowledgments..xvii

About the Author..xvii

I Starting Your Career in Cybersecurity   1

  1 The Cybersecurity Universe.......................................3

  2 Establishing a Plan...25

  3 Building Your Lab...45

  4 Networking...65

  5 Interview..83

II On the Job   97

  6 Your Employer Is Your Customer..................................99

  7 Dealing with Obstacles...111

  8 Growing in Your Career as a Remote Worker......................127

  9 What's Next in Your Career?....................................139

  10 Owning a Cybersecurity Business...............................149

     Index...161

TABLE OF CONTENTS

Foreword xiv

Introduction xv

Acknowledgments xvii

About the Author xvii

I   STARTING YOUR CAREER IN CYBERSECURITY 1

1   The Cybersecurity Universe   3

Cybersecurity Careers 4

Cybersecurity Roles and Responsibilities 5

Cybersecurity Jobs 8

Cybersecurity Skills 12

Navigating the Industry 17

Summary 23

2   Establishing a Plan   25

Explore Your Current Skills 26

Create Your Plan 30

Organizing Your Plan 32

Cybersecurity Certifications 34

Foundational Security Certifications 36

Cybersecurity Analyst and Security Practitioners
Certifications 40

Specializations 42

Vendor-Specific Certifications 43

Summary 44

3   Building Your Lab   45

Lab Requirements 46

Creating Your Lab 49

Scenario 1—Operating Systems Process 49

Scenario 2—Network Traffic Analysis 52

Scenario 3—Cloud Security Posture Management 56

Scenario 4—Multi-Cloud Security 57

Scenario 5—Regulatory Compliance 57

Scenario 6—Attack Simulation................................ 57

Scenario 7—Security Information and Event
Management... 58

Scenario 8—Threat Hunting.................................. 59

Scenario 9—Threat Intelligence............................ 59

Self-Assessment... 60

Summary.. 63

4   Networking   65

Networking in Cybersecurity.............................. 66

Look Inward.. 69

Online Presence.. 73

LinkedIn.. 74

YouTube.. 75

Twitter.. 76

Searching for a Job... 77

Summary.. 82

5   Interview   83

Technical and soft skills..................................... 84

Interview process.. 84

Initial triage.. 85

Prepare for the interview................................ 85

Formal interview rounds................................. 88

Interview questions..................................... 90

Final decision.. 93

Summary.. 95

II   ON THE JOB   97

6   Your Employer Is Your Customer   99

Cybersecurity Goes Beyond Technology................. 100

Organizational Structure................................. 102

Responsibilities and Expectations..................... 103

Mapping Your Responsibilities....................... 104

Plan to Conquer... 105

Entrepreneur Mindset 106

Summary 109

7　Dealing with Obstacles　111

Obstacles in Cybersecurity 112

Unconscious Bias and Cybersecurity 115

Adjusting Your Cybersecurity Skills 117

What Got You Here Won't Get You There 119

Work-Life Balance in Cybersecurity 119

Growing at a Healthy Pace 122

Time Management 124

Summary 126

8　Growing in Your Career as a Remote Worker　127

The Growth of Remote Workers 128

Hybrid Work 130

Making an Impact as a Remote Worker 131

Influencing Others 132

Actively Look for Feedback 133

Staying Active 134

Transparency 136

Summary 137

9　What's Next in Your Career?　139

Moving Up or Moving Laterally? 140

Self-Assessment 142

Evaluating the Options 143

Upcoming Cybersecurity Opportunities 144

Keep Moving Forward 148

Summary 148

10   Owning a Cybersecurity Business   149

Knowing More about the Guest Authors 150

Stepping Stones to Flying Solo 152

Paula Januszkiewicz's Keys to Entrepreneurial Success 153

　Key Elements for Success 154

　Common Pitfalls and Challenges 156

David Kennedy: Starting from the Ground Up 158

　Final Considerations 160

Summary 160

Index 161

Foreword

We live in a world where cybersecurity events are daily, front-page news — zero-day vulnerabilities in software supply chains, stolen credentials, attacks on hospitals, gas pipeline shut-downs, and school ransomware events. As we've become a more digital and connected global economy, the number of attacks has increased with no sign of slowing down. The need for people working in cybersecurity has never been more acute.

While my background as a cybersecurity leader is more traditional, coming from both military and engineering, I actually began my career in information technology. However, early on, I realized the huge potential of the cybersecurity industry, fell in love with the mission, and developed a great passion for the domain. There is no one path to the field. In fact, there are many ways to get started, whether your background is in engineering, education, law, criminal justice, marketing, sales, finance, or human resources.

You could be part of a technology startup like Dazz, which builds innovative products and services to help organizations discover, reduce, and fix security risks. For women, in particular, who have low representation in cyber, I encourage you to join startups in their early stages, when most of the learning takes place.

Alternatively, you could be a practitioner and get hands-on with technology or intelligence as a cybercrime investigator, ethical hacker, red team tester, researcher, security architect, or information security leader inside a company, school, hospital, or government.

Whichever path you take, you'll stretch and grow, learn new things, and gain fulfillment knowing you are working for the greater good of society.

You are in good hands with my friend and colleague, Yuri Diogenes, on how to begin your journey. There is high demand for skilled cybersecurity professionals, which is only expected to grow in the coming years. I encourage you to join us and experience one of the most rewarding careers you could embark upon.

Merav Bahat
Co-founder and CEO
Dazz

Introduction

Coming from a background in information technology, and more specifically, computer networks, the migration to cybersecurity was very smooth because I had a good foundation in two critical areas: operating systems and networking. However, I didn't understand the options available in this field or what gaps I needed to fulfill before applying for a cybersecurity-related position. I had no idea where to start. To this day, I believe I spent too much time focusing on the wrong things, and my cybersecurity career took a little longer to take off. In addition to my personal experience entering this field back in 2006, I keep seeing a trend among my university students who frequently ask for guidance on either improving in this field (if they are already in cybersecurity) or how to migrate from a different area to cybersecurity. These trends not only match my own experience but also match common questions brought to me by my mentees at work.

Based on these experiences, I decided to start this project, and when I was writing the table of contents for the book, I also reflected on the areas I took for granted but were critical in my career growth, such as soft skills. I decided to frame the book so that it is not only about cybersecurity per se but how to be a complete cybersecurity professional who can add value to the business, both from a technology and overall package perspective. As a manager in my company, I see many candidates hired because they were complete candidates — soft skills, attitude, mindset, and technical abilities — not because they had the best technology resumes.

My experience as a cybersecurity professional, university professor, and manager has allowed me to share different dimensions of what it takes to build a solid career in cybersecurity. However, I wanted to ensure that I had the right team to be part of this project, so I invited Nicholas DiCola, VP of Zero Networks and my former manager at Microsoft, to be the technical reviewer for the book. Nicholas has a lot of experience in this field, and throughout this project, he gave me extra tips to include in the book. I also invited Merav Bahat, co-founder and CEO of Dazz, a cloud security startup, to assist. I worked with Merav at Microsoft, where she was directly responsible for my career growth to the next level. I also wanted to incorporate some entrepreneurship vision to show that you can start your own cybersecurity business, so I invited Paula Januszkiewicz and David Kennedy to lend their perspectives. Paula and David are two great cybersecurity professionals with their own cybersecurity businesses.

I hope that the hours we invested in this book are valuable to you and you can finish this book with a good plan of action to pursue your cybersecurity career and become a better professional.

Good luck!

Yuri Diogenes

Register your copy of *Building a Career in Cybersecurity* on the InformIT site for convenient access to updates and/or corrections as they become available. To start the registration process, go to informit.com/register and log in or create an account. Enter the product ISBN (9780138214517) and click Submit. Look on the Registered Products tab for an Access Bonus Content link next to this product, and follow that link to access any available bonus materials. If you would like to be notified of exclusive offers on new editions and updates, please check the box to receive email from us.

Acknowledgments

I would like to thank my wife and daughters for their endless support; my great God for giving me strength and guiding my path on each step of the way. Thanks to my mother, for always emphasizing to me the importance of education and study. To my coworkers and former managers that contributed to my career progress, especially Cyndee Young, Rebecca Halla, and Sonia Wadhwa.

I want to thank my friend Nicholas DiCola for the great work reviewing this book, friendship, and guidance over the years. Thanks to Merav Bahat for writing the foreword of this book and for her inspiring career and leadership. Thanks to my friends Paula Januszkiewicz and David Kennedy for your amazing contributions to Chapter 10. Thanks for bringing your vision and valuable insights. I truly appreciate it.

Thanks to Pearson's team, especially Loretta Yates and Rick Kughen, for another amazing partnership.

About the Author

Yuri Diogenes has a master of science in cybersecurity intelligence and forensics investigation from UTICA College and is working on his Ph.D. in cybersecurity leadership from Capitol Technology University. Yuri has been working at Microsoft since 2006 and is a principal PM manager for the Customer Experience Engineering Defender for Cloud team, where he manages a global team of product managers focusing on cloud security posture management and workload protection. Yuri has published more than 30 books, mostly about information security and Microsoft technologies. Yuri is also a professor at EC-Council University, where he teaches in the cybersecurity bachelor's program. Yuri also has an MBA and many IT/Security industry certifications, such as CISSP, MITRE ATT&CK Cyber Threat Intelligence Certified, E|CND, E|CEH, E|CSA, E|CHFI, CompTIA Security+, CySA+, Network+, CASP, and CyberSec First Responder. You can follow Yuri on Twitter at @yuridiogenes.

Starting Your Career in Cybersecurity

1 The Cybersecurity Universe 1

2 Establishing a Plan 25

3 Building Your Lab 45

4 Networking 65

5 Interview 83

1

The Cybersecurity Universe

"Change is the law of life. And those who look only to the past or present are certain to miss the future."

–John F. Kennedy

One common question I have received over the years while teaching, mentoring, or guiding someone to grow in their career is, "Should I change my career to focus on cybersecurity?" This is a very personal question because I believe changing careers should be motivated by a desire to find your passion. So, I answered the question with more questions:

- Why are you trying to change your career?
- What do you know about cybersecurity?
- Why do you think cybersecurity is a good fit for you?

To better answer these questions, you need to know more about cybersecurity and the different roles available in this field. Nowadays, saying that you work in "cyber-security" is as generic as saying, "I'm a Medical Doctor" because the next question is always, "What's your specialty?" The universe of cybersecurity has different fields of expertise. In other words, chances are you will identify your passion in one of these specialty areas, but you need to explore the options available before chang-ing careers. This chapter provides an initial assessment of the cybersecurity field, enabling you to plan your next steps. It is time to make some changes!

Cybersecurity Careers

According to the *(ISC) Cybersecurity Workforce Study 2022*, despite the addition of 464,000 cybersecurity workers in the previous year, there is still a worldwide gap of 3.4 million cybersecurity workers. The organizations fully know what this means to them, and 70 percent admitted that they don't have enough cybersecurity staff to be effective. However, 43 percent of these organizations do not hire qualified cyberse-curity talent.

 Note

You can download the PDF for this study at *https://www.isc2.org/Research/Workforce-Study*.

I could reference dozens more articles to emphasize this cybersecurity talent short-age, but let's focus on what this really means to you and how you can navigate the available options.

Cybersecurity Roles and Responsibilities

If you are new to cybersecurity, it will be harder to understand where you can fit in and which job is ideal for you. For this reason, it is important to better understand how cybersecurity roles and responsibilities work at an organizational level.

When you are hired to work in a cybersecurity job, you will be part of a team with a specific set of responsibilities to fulfill. This team is often part of a bigger organization that overarches the entire security strategy and operations for the company. On top of this hierarchy sits the chief security officer (CSO), but in some companies, this role may be called the head of security or vice president (VP/SVP) of security.

Different security functions require people to fulfill different types of cybersecurity jobs based on a set of skills. Though the granularity of these functions and how they reflect the security team hierarchy varies by company, Microsoft has observed some patterns regarding roles and responsibilities over the years. Table 1.1 shows the most common security functions and typical job roles.

 Note

For more information, see *The evolution of cybersecurity roles and responsibilities* at *https://www.microsoft.com/en-us/security/blog/2020/08/06/organize-security-team-evolution-cybersecurity-roles-responsibilities/*.

Table 1.1 Security functions

Function	Description	Job roles
Policy and standards	Responsible for authoring policy and standards based on the company security strategy, including using regulatory compliance standards, establishing baselines, and industry best practices.	• Cybersecurity architect • Compliance analyst • Information technology (IT) analyst
Network security	Responsible for the network security infrastructure, including network security architecture, network segmentation and design.	• Network security professional • Network security architect

Function	Description	Job roles
Security operations center (SOC)	Responsible for detecting, responding, and remediating active attacks on the company's assets.	• SOC analyst • Intrusion detection analyst • IT operations • Incident responder (IR) engineer • Computer forensics analyst
Threat Intelligence	Responsible for providing actionable intelligence related to active threats that can empower organizational leaders and teams to make better decisions and protect the company.	• Threat intelligence analyst • Threat hunter • Open-source intelligence (OSINT) analyst
Cloud security architecture	Responsible for ensuring the right level of visibility and control across all cloud assets.	• Cloud security architect • Cloud security analyst • IT architect • Cybersecurity analyst
Application security and DevOps	Responsible for integrating security assurances into development processes. It may also include defining and implementing a shift-left strategy and security development lifecycle.	• Security engineer • Software engineer (developer) • DevSecOps engineer • Cloud security analyst • Infrastructure security analyst • Application security engineer
Data security	Responsible for implementing protective and detective controls for sensitive data within the organization.	• Data protection analyst • Data privacy analyst • Data protection and compliance analyst • Data architect

Function	Description	Job roles
Infrastructure and endpoint security	Responsible for security protection of the infrastructure (on-premises and cloud), including servers and endpoints.	• Cloud security analyst • Security engineer • Endpoint security analyst • Endpoint security architect
Posture management	Responsible for the posture management strategy, including the cloud environment. It may also include vulnerability assessment and management.	• Vulnerability management analyst • Infrastructure vulnerability management specialist • Cybersecurity engineer–vulnerability management • Cloud security engineer
Red team	Responsible for performing controlled attacks against the infrastructure to identify security gaps before threat actors do.	• Penetrator tester (also called pen tester) • Malware engineer • Malware reverse engineer • Security researcher
Blue team	Responsible for establishing security controls and defense strategies across the environment.	• Security analyst • Cybersecurity analyst • Security researcher • Security engineer

The information shown in Table 1.1 is just an example of some of the most common functions and job roles, and as you can see, you can specialize in many areas. If you are migrating from information technology to cybersecurity, you may see some of your skills across different areas, so you need to start thinking about how your current skills can be leveraged to accelerate your ramp-up in this new field.

If you are completely new to cybersecurity without an information technology background, you can start fresh and choose which area is most exciting for you.

Cybersecurity Jobs

As you can see in the previous section, there are many specializations in cybersecurity to choose from. These specializations will dictate two important aspects:

- The type of cybersecurity job
- The skills required

Understanding the type of job you will need to do is an important step, because this is a way to understand the daily tasks and how exciting this job could be. This is an important decision in your career, which means you must be very mindful of what this job is about.

- Do you think you will have fun?
- Do you think you will enjoy it?
- Do you think that this type of job will challenge you to continue growing?

These are not secondary questions. In fact, during the 2005 Stanford graduation ceremony, Steve Jobs said, "The only way to do great work is to love what you do." He is right about that—not only because of his personal experience but because many studies bear this out.

A fascinating 11-year longitudinal study published in the *Journal of Applied Psychology* suggests that when you are passionate about your work, you have more chances to take actions that will drive you to grow and be successful. That's why when I receive vague questions, such as, "Yuri, do you think I should change my career to start working with cybersecurity?" my answer is always, "I don't know." This is because I really don't know what this person is passionate about, and I won't advise someone to move to a career without knowing more about their skills and aspirations.

Before digging more into the different cybersecurity job roles, it is important to call out some important facts about cybersecurity job titles:

- The cybersecurity job titles I will mention in this book are based on the most common cybersecurity job titles in the United States. Most of the titles used in this book are part of the *20 Coolest Careers in Cybersecurity* article by SysAdmin, Audit, Network, and Security (SANS). You may see different job titles—or even titles not shown in this book—because covering all the potential titles available worldwide is practically impossible.

- The job title may have fundamental differences depending on the company size. In small organizations, a cybersecurity analyst may be required to perform tasks that were supposed to be done by a pen tester or cyberoperations specialist. However, since the company doesn't have the budget to segment its operations, it will hire one person to perform multiple unrelated tasks within information security. This is most common in small to medium organizations.

- The geographic location also plays an important factor. I am from Brazil, and during my first 10 years working in the IT industry there and interacting with other professionals from South America, I could see the behavior described in the previous bullet. However, it often wasn't because of the company's smaller budget. Instead, it was more a cultural aspect of the South American region, where there is the expectation that you will do way more than the job title really entails.

 Note

You can read more and download the poster for these jobs at *https://www.sans.org/cybersecurity-careers/20-coolest-cyber-security-careers/*.

For all these reasons, it is important to always read the job description carefully. Some companies are more explicit regarding the tasks a candidate is expected to do. Figure 1.1 shows a LinkedIn search for "cybersecurity analyst." (The *senior security operations analyst* job description is what a cybersecurity analyst does, even though the title is different.)

LinkedIn will be covered more in-depth in Chapter 4. For now, focus on reading the description of what needs to be done (the "Work you'll do" section shown in Figure 1.1). Think about it and answer these questions:

- Does this sound exciting to me?

- Do I see myself doing this job and enjoying my daily tasks?

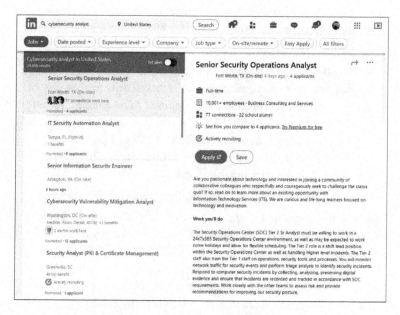

Figure 1.1 *LinkedIn job search example*

If you answered "no" to both, don't waste time; move on to check the next job post. If you answered "yes" to both, then continue reading the job post, particularly the job requirements.

Job requirements are usually divided into two sections: basic qualifications and preferred qualifications. However, this can vary according to how the company's human resources (HR) department requires the hiring manager to write the job description. Figure 1.2 shows an example of the job requirements for the position shown previously in Figure 1.1.

Here is where you really need to be honest with yourself and ask, "Do I have these qualifications?" Don't lie to yourself. Perform an honest self-assessment and apply only if you meet the basic qualifications.

Don't get me wrong. You can always apply for any job you want, even if you don't have the basic qualifications. However, if you don't have the qualifications, applying will be a shot in the dark, and you're probably wasting your time by hoping it will somehow work out.

Figure 1.2 *Job requirements*

1:1 WITH THE AUTHOR: INCREASE YOUR CHANCES OF BEING INTERVIEWED

You may not realize this, but writing a job description, posting, screening, and interviewing is a lot of work for the hiring manager. I say that because I've done this many times, and it never gets easier. The entire process can take weeks, and the initial screening process is one of the most important ones because it is there that you will decide who will go through the interview loop.

In 2022, I posted a job on the company's career website on a Monday, and by Wednesday, I already had 250 applicants, dozens of internal emails asking for informational meetings, and multiple chat requests on Teams asking to talk about the job. When reviewing all those 250 applicants, we need to review what we have: the resume. I needed to look at the candidates' qualifications and experience to see if they matched the job requirements. If it didn't match, I moved on to the next one. Out of 250 applications, I filtered them to seven candidates for the first round of interviews and then culled them to three applicants for the final round.

The tip here is that if you are interested in a particular position, you need to format your resume to highlight what you believe will be important for that job. People often keep a steady resume and use the same one for multiple jobs—and sometimes completely unrelated jobs. If you have the skills and experience you are applying for, make sure you capitalize on that by updating your resume to highlight those points. You want to pass through that initial screening filter and earn the chance to be interviewed. Chances are you won't be selected if your resume doesn't highlight your strengths related to the preferred qualifications for the job you are applying for.

In summary:

- Keep your resume up to date

- Keep it simple (one or two pages)

- Highlight your expertise, experience, and qualifications

Another important point about the job posting is the position tenure. When you see a position like the one shown in Figure 1.1 (senior security operations analyst), there is an expectation that the candidate already has vast experience working in this area. In other words, this is not the type of job that a fresh-out-of-college candidate without work-related experience will apply for and expect to succeed. Again, you must be honest with yourself to avoid creating false expectations. Many entry-level cybersecurity positions are available to absorb these types of candidates.

Cybersecurity Skills

If you are new to cybersecurity but have a background in information technology, you definitely have the advantage of inheriting some of the necessary technical skills to help you with a quicker ramp-up in cybersecurity. If you are moving from a different field to start over in cybersecurity, don't worry that it will take forever to digest the basics before starting your job search. Your success depends on your level of dedication and commitment to speeding up your ramp-up process.

Minimum Technical Skills Required

The technical skills necessary for a cybersecurity job will vary according to the position, though some basic technical skills are recommended before you start diving into more details on the technical cybersecurity jargon.

Use Table 1.2 as a self-assessment tool to mark what you need to learn and what you already know. The "Desired Knowledge Level to Start" column suggests the minimum level you should have in these topics before studying specific cybersecurity-related terminologies. In the "Current Knowledge Level" column, enter your current knowledge level using the numbering system below:

- **100:** Very basic level of understanding. You know what the terminology means, but you don't know how to explain in detail how it works.

- **200:** Medium level of understanding. You already feel more comfortable explaining how certain technology works.

- **300:** Advanced level of understanding. You have more than a theoretical understanding of the topic, but you have already implemented the technology.

- **400:** Expert level of understanding. You dominate the topic and can be considered a subject matter expert (SME).

Table 1.2   Technical skills self-assessment

Topic	Description	Desired Starting Knowledge	Current Knowledge Level
Operating system	Understand operating systems (Windows and Linux) core architecture, including key concepts such as process, threads, network communication, authentication, and authorization.	200	
Computer networks	Understand how computer networks work, including TCP/IP protocol stack (transport protocol, Internet protocol, and communication ports).	200	
Directory services	Understand what a directory service is and how it is used to authenticate and authorize users.	100	
Encryption	Understand the purpose of encryption, know the difference between symmetric and asymmetric encryption, and know the use case scenarios for each.	100	
Cloud computing	Understand the principles of cloud computing, the different service models, and how they can be used.	100	

Topic	Description	Desired Start-ing Knowledge	Current Knowledge Level
Application development	Understand the principles of application development, script-ing, DevOps, and development lifecycle.	100	

As you can see in Table 1.2, operating systems and networks are the only two top-ics in which I think you should have a 200-level (or better) understanding before applying for cybersecurity jobs. In my experience mentoring professionals over the years, operating systems and computer networks are the two most critical topics to learn before entering the cybersecurity field.

As much as you might believe you can skip all these steps and start "hacking things," the reality is that as you learn more about cybersecurity, there will be moments when things won't make sense. Usually, that happens when you are miss-ing the basics—and the basics are operating systems and computer networks. For this reason, many IT professionals with many years of experience in infrastructure or system administration will ramp up more quickly in cybersecurity because they already have the basics to build upon.

If you are migrating from a different field and only use computers for email, you need to create your roadmap for learning those skills. In the next chapter, you will learn how to do that.

Soft Skills

While you might think that all you need is to be technically savvy to get a new job in cybersecurity, the reality is that employers are always looking beyond the techni-cality, and soft skills are extremely important not only to get you started but also to allow you to continue to grow in the company. Regardless of your technical ability, you need to know how to collaborate and work in an environment where you feel good about sharing what you know and can be coachable. You won't be able to suc-ceed if you are difficult to work with or impose your opinions without considering others' opinions.

Generally, the technical questions will come later in the interview process when determining whether your approach to tackling problems will add value to the team. For example, potential cybersecurity employers want to know the following:

- Is this person someone who seeks assistance or tries to resolve prob-lems independently?

- Is this person good at receiving feedback?

- Is this person coachable?

So, what are some important soft skills to have in cybersecurity? The list below can apply to any job, but successful cybersecurity professionals usually have these skills:

- **Growth mindset:** This is an important cybersecurity skill because of the dynamic threat landscape. Things are always changing, and if you have a fixed mindset, you will have difficulty adapting to new challenges and identifying how to overcome them. Adaptability comes as part of a growth mindset; you will need this as a cybersecurity professional.

- **Being coachable**: Don't assume you know everything, even if you have 400-level knowledge in an area. Be humble and look for mentorship to keep improving. Being coachable is very important and highly appreciated by senior leaders in the company because they see your effort to be always improving.

- **Critical thinking**: There's often no absolute answer for everything in cybersecurity. Sometimes, things aren't black and white; they're gray. If you are absolute in your approach, you will struggle to find a middle ground in some scenarios. Critical thinking is a must-have in this field.

- **Effective communication**: In today's hybrid work environment, effective communication (online meetings, email, text, and in-person) is critical. You will often not be able to use your body language to express yourself, which means you must rely only on the clarity of your writing skills. As a cybersecurity professional, you must be able to clearly communicate with a wide range of people, from the end user to the company's chief security officer.

- **Inclusivity and empathy**: Many "old school" security professionals tend to blame users for issues that occur when they call for help. This mindset can be a problem for cybersecurity professionals because they become biased by their own assumptions that the problem is with the user. You must be inclusive of other people's ideas and backgrounds. You must listen while avoiding bias and be empathetic to someone's situation. All those things will influence how you view and tackle problems.

- **Collaboration**: There is nothing worse than collaborating with someone who doesn't like sharing knowledge or is always trying to hide important information to appear as the only one who knows a specific topic. To be successful in cybersecurity, you must collaborate with others to help the company be more secure. If you have a hard time collaborating, you better start changing now.

- **Delegation:** Even the most experienced professionals struggle to delegate tasks. Julius Caesar, a Roman general and politician, often used the divide-and-conquer strategy to win battles, even when relying on his subordinates to follow his vision and strategy. That's how you should think about the delegation of activities. You will conquer more because you can only do so much on your own. If you learn how to delegate, you can achieve more. By making others accountable to complete tasks, you are not only helping the overall team to make progress, but you are also enabling another professional to own a task and develop new skills. Because of the amount of work that needs to be done to improve a company's security, knowing how to delegate becomes extremely critical to a cybersecurity professional.

You can explore the soft skills mentioned above by checking out specialized books detailing how to improve your skills in these areas. I mention them here to provide a framework for determining where you need to invest more in developing soft skills that will positively affect your cybersecurity career.

1:1 WITH THE AUTHOR: SOFT SKILLS DURING THE INTERVIEW

Before moving to the technical interview rounds, the interviewer must determine whether you are a good fit for the company and team and will embrace the company's culture. In my experience interviewing candidates for cybersecurity jobs, this is where many people fail and don't even get a chance to make it to the technical rounds.

I've seen many cases over the years where the most prepared professional from the technical standpoint didn't get the position because their soft skills were weak and full of red flags. Although sometimes a candidate is super-talented from a technical perspective, they might not be a good fit for the team. The rationale is that training someone to excel technically is easier than changing someone's character and attitude. That's why that first impression during the interview is so important.

It doesn't take too much effort to quickly identify whether the candidate is a good fit, particularly if there are red flags along the way. That's why it is so important for you to embody these soft skills and incorporate them in your current job, even before moving to the next job. You need to practice those skills and become proficient in using them. It is hard to play someone you aren't or memorize just enough to make it through an interview. During the interview, you might be asked to share some of your previous experience using a skill you don't possess. For example, the interviewer may pose a question like, "Tell me about a scenario where you used critical thinking to resolve a challenging problem and how you effectively communicated that to the stakeholders."

This type of question needs to be answered with authority. Either you lived that situation, or you didn't. If you try to come up with a fictitious scenario, it will be easy to identify if it is real. Also, remember that the interviewer might ask follow-up questions, so bringing real-world experience is imperative for your success.

Navigating the Industry

One of the biggest advantages of cybersecurity compared with other careers is that all medium to large organizations will need a dedicated in-house information security team to help them stay safe. This means the opportunities in this field are vast across all industries. Table 1.1 provides a backdrop for different security-related functions within a company and the available roles. Most likely, at least one of those roles will be available in the industry that you aim to work for.

The Cyber Seek Heatmap shown in Figure 1.3 is one tool you can use to explore the opportunities available in each state. (When this chapter was written, the Cyber Seek Heatmap was only available for the United States market.) The Cyber Seek Heatmap is sponsored by Lightcast (a leading job skills authority), CompTIA (a leading vendor-neutral IT certifying body), and The National Initiative for Cybersecurity Education (NICE), which is led by the National Institute of Standards and Technology (NIST).

 Note

You can access this tool by visiting *https://www.cyberseek.org/heatmap.html*.

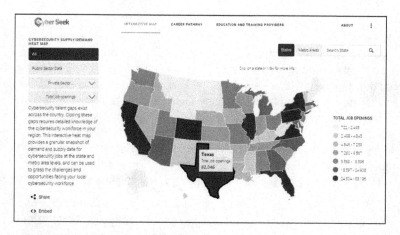

Figure 1.3 *Cyber Seek Heatmap*

This site allows you to narrow your search per state, see the available opportunities there, and filter per sector (public and private). If you scroll down on this page, you can also see the cybersecurity jobs available per framework category and the top job tiles, as shown in Figure 1.4.

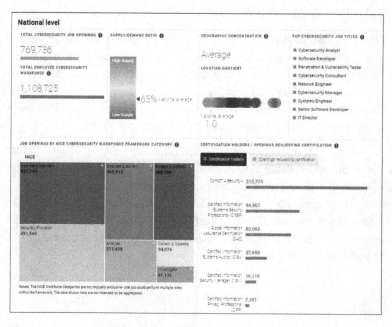

Figure 1.4 *More insights about cybersecurity jobs*

With this information, you can determine where you may see more future opportunities for your desired job title. Keep in mind that salaries will vary according to the cost of living in a specific geographic location, meaning a cybersecurity analyst may have a bigger compensation package in California compared to the same job position in the same company in another state. This includes remote workers, too. Even though you will be working remotely, you will still be earning the compensation package crafted for where you live and work from, not where the company is located.

Working in Cybersecurity for Big Techs

While there are many opportunities to work in cybersecurity across different industries, there are also plenty of cybersecurity jobs available in the "big techs." For this book, I'll highlight Microsoft, Google, Meta (Facebook), and Amazon Web Services (AWS). The interesting part of working at a big tech is that you can follow the same job roles presented in Table 1.1 and work for the company's information security organization, or you can be part of the team that creates their security products.

This ramification opens a whole new universe of possibilities for working in cybersecurity. The *Glassdoor.com* website can help you learn more about each company and even compare the benefits of each. This site has very accurate information about many companies because people that work in those companies are the ones doing the reviews. You will find a lot of interesting data about compensation packages and salary ranges within each position. You can also use this tool to compare companies using many parameters, including employee ratings, as shown in Figure 1.5.

Product management is a very common job title because these companies create products. While the product manager (PM) job title can mean many things depending on the team, cybersecurity jobs are available within product management.

Companies like Microsoft and Google have teams dedicated to creating security products, so they will have different types of cybersecurity-related jobs available, and you must think about a product's lifecycle and how you could fit in. Figure 1.6 shows the different areas in which cybersecurity-related roles might be available at a company that produces security products.

Figure 1.5 *Comparing companies using Glassdoor.*

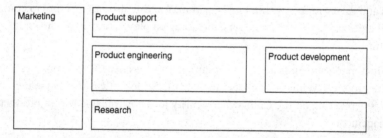

Figure 1.6 *Areas that can have cybersecurity opportunities*

While Figure 1.6 is not a definitive org chart, it provides some foundational areas that usually exist in a company that commercializes security-related products. Now let's map these areas with the potential cybersecurity opportunities in Table 1.3.

The point of this exercise is to open your mind to understanding that not all cyber-security-related positions will have "cybersecurity" or "security" in the title. That's why it's so important for you to read the job description and not just the job title. When you just scan through job titles, you may miss a great opportunity to work in cybersecurity but with a different job title. Make sure to also read the job respon-sibilities section (if one is available) to understand what the daily job looks like because the job title often does not reflect what you will be doing daily.

Table 1.3 Cybersecurity opportunities

Area	Potential cybersecurity job	Role description
Marketing	Marketing program manager Product marketing manager	Despite the generic title, this role within the security product organization requires a basic understanding of the cybersecurity industry to help with marketing campaigns for the product. For example, a company with a Cloud Security Posture Management solution needs a go-to-market strategy that considers the current cybersecurity threats and how this product will address them.
Product support	Support engineer Customer engineer	This is another generic title, but when linked to the organization that builds the security product, the professional must have a deep technical knowledge of the product and at least a 200-level understanding of cybersecurity.
Product engineering	Product manager Program manager Technical product manager	This role requires a deep understanding of translating customers' needs into product specs. When developing a security-related product, it also becomes necessary to understand the threat landscape and the security capabilities that must be included in the product.
Product development	Software engineer Developer	This role is deep on coding. Although cybersecurity knowledge is not a must-have for most of these roles, having it is a big advantage. In an organization that creates security products, developers who know how to use the security development lifecyle and write secure code have an advantage over regular developers.
Research	Researcher	The interesting part of this role is that the title is usually tailored to the discipline of the organization. For example, if you are working for an organization that is responsible for creating a cloud security product, then having security researchers on the team is very likely required.

 Tip

The *Cracking the PM Interview* video is a great resource that you can use to familiarize yourself with the PM role and what potential questions you may receive during a PM interview. See *https://youtu.be/CshJxTcsgvo*.

1:1 WITH THE AUTHOR: IS CYBERSECURITY A GOOD FIT FOR ME?

Although there is a lot to digest in this chapter, you should at least have a good idea of the different cybersecurity opportunities by now. Honestly, the only person who can answer whether cybersecurity is a good fit for YOU. While this book can open your eyes to different opportunities, you must be very sincere in evaluating the pros and cons of moving to this field.

It is important to understand why you are moving to this field. Without the "why," it becomes hard to evaluate your progress down the road. Ask yourself a simple question: Why am I trying to switch to this field? The answer to this question will give you a good foundation to build upon.

Throughout the years of mentoring IT Professionals who wanted to move to cybersecurity, I've seen different motivations for this migration, and I can certainly say that the professionals who were more successful after the migration were the ones that had one thing in common: *they were passionate about cybersecurity*.

I've met many professionals motivated by money—not a passion for cybersecurity—who did not go far in cybersecurity. This field can be challenging, requires dedication, and is very humbling because it constantly reminds you that you have more to learn. Not everyone is ready to be comfortable in uncomfortable situations, and the cybersecurity field often puts you in uncomfortable situations. If you are not passionate about those things and money is your only motivation, you can go for it, but beware that it will be very challenging to keep growing in your career in the long run.

If you are migrating from a completely different field, you should also perform this self-assessment and reflect on your "why." You can always start in one area of cybersecurity and move to a different one. For example, maybe your first job was in a security operations center (SOC), and while you learned a lot, you didn't really like the hectic nature of the business and wanted to change to something more strategic and proactive rather than reactive. There is nothing wrong with that, and this is the amazing thing about a cybersecurity career: there are different flavors, and chances are that you will find one you like.

Summary

In this chapter, you learned about the different aspects of careers in cybersecurity. You learned about the job roles and responsibilities, the current demand for cybersecurity professionals, and the necessary technical and soft skills to work in cybersecurity. You learned more about the different opportunities available in the industry and the cybersecurity opportunities in the big techs. In the next chapter, you will establish your plan for learning about cybersecurity.

2

Establishing a Plan

"An hour of planning can save you 10 hours of doing."

–Dale Carnegie

Now that you have a foundational understanding of the different aspects of a cybersecurity career, you need to have a good plan that will lead you to achieve your desired goal.

One of the most common mistakes I've seen with many professionals who were migrating from other fields (such as IT) to cybersecurity is trying to absorb everything at once instead of following a well-thought-out plan that will not only lead to the accomplishment of their final goal but also enable them to have multiple "check-ins" to track progress over time.

A key element of a career plan is to recognize your current skill set, map your current gaps and understand your current constraints. People often cannot afford to take time off to focus on acquiring new skills via training or self-learning. That's when having a solid plan can help you to better manage your time according to your current workload. This chapter will assist you in creating this plan, demonstrate how you can track your progress, and cover the aspect of professional certifications.

Explore Your Current Skills

In Chapter 1, you learned about the desirable skills for different cybersecurity roles, the desirable level, and a quick self-assessment to understand your current knowledge in those areas. Now you need to dig deeper to see if there are gaps to fill regarding foundational concepts and terminologies.

As I wrote this chapter, a friend who works in marketing and is trying to transition to cybersecurity sent an article to me titled "Bitwarden password vaults targeted in Google ads phishing attack." His email read: "I'm a bit lost on this article because I don't understand what a phishing campaign is. Can you please clarify?"

 Note

See "Bitwarden password vaults targeted in Google ads phishing attack" at *https://www.bleepingcomputer.com/news/security/ bitwarden-password-vaults-targeted-in-google-ads-phishing-attack/*.

I applauded him for admitting that he didn't understand the term and asking for help. You might think this is standard behavior, but unfortunately, it is not. Many people avoid asking what they think are basic questions to avoid being judged as someone who doesn't know the basic concepts. Don't do that. As you migrate to cybersecurity, you will learn that asking questions is literally part of the job. Never move on until you have a full understanding of the terminology.

This article outlines some key terminology to help you avoid getting lost as you read about cybersecurity. This article will help you perform an initial assessment and identify areas in which you need to improve.

 TIP

When reading an article containing terminology you don't understand, make sure to write those terms down. Figure 2.1 shows a marked-up article. These notes will help you identify gaps in your understanding.

 Note

See "CISA: Federal agencies hacked using legitimate remote desktop tools" at *https://www.bleepingcomputer.com/news/security/cisa-federal-agencies-hacked-using-legitimate-remote-desktop-tools/*.

They also provided a list of measures designed to help mitigate such risks and ensure that networks are secure from incoming attack attempts.

To protect against potential security breaches, companies and organizations should audit installed remote access tools and identify authorized RMM software.

The use of application controls to prevent the execution of unauthorized RMM software and only utilizing authorized RMM software over approved remote access solutions, such as VPN or VDI, is also recommended, as is blocking both inbound and outbound connections on standard RMM ports and protocols.

To further enhance security, organizations should implement training programs and phishing exercises to raise awareness among their employees about the risks linked to phishing and spearphishing emails.

Figure 2.1 *Article from bleepingcomputer.com*

You might have heard many of those terms because they are becoming mainstream. However, do you really know the essence of that terminology? Let's use the term "VPN" as an example. You know what a VPN does and what VPN stands for (virtual private network), but do you know how the technology really works? Figure 2.2 shows a basic VPN setup diagram. Can you identify what each component is doing?

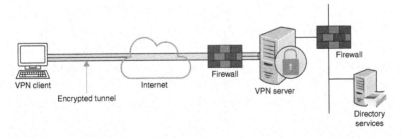

Figure 2.2 *Basic VPN*

Review this diagram and answer the following questions:

- How was this encrypted tunnel established?

- If VPN is secure, why is a firewall in front of the VPN server?

- Why is another firewall behind the VPN server?

- What is the role of the directory services in this VPN architecture?

Take a few minutes to think through these questions and then compare your answers to the answers below:

- **How was this encrypted tunnel established?**

  - **Answer:** The VPN client established a secure connection with the VPN server using a secure protocol, such as IP Security (IPSec). IPSec uses the IKE (Internet Key Exchange) protocol to negotiate and establish a secure connection between the VPN client and server. The VPN client and server must use compatible protocols and parameters for the connection to be successfully established.

- **If VPN is secure, why is a firewall in front of the VPN server?**

  - **Answer:** The goal of the edge firewall—the firewall that sits between the public network (Internet) and the internal network—is to ensure that only specific ports and protocols can be reachable. In other words, access to most of the connection requests is denied; only a certain type of connection is allowed.

- **Why is another firewall behind the VPN server?**

  - **Answer:** The VPN server is usually located in a DMZ (demilitarized zone), an isolated network with restricted access to shared services. The internal firewall ensures that only certain requests can reach the internal network.

- **What is the role of the directory services in this VPN architecture?**

  - **Answer:** For the VPN connection to be successfully established, the user must authenticate using their credentials. In this case, the directory service will be used to authenticate the user.

Can you answer those questions without researching the answers? If so, you have a good foundational understanding of how a VPN works. However, this is not only about cybersecurity; many elements in this scenario are core computer network topics. Figure 2.3 shows a topic map organized by domain to explain how the subject expands to multiple areas.

Figure 2.3 *Beyond cybersecurity*

The purpose of the diagram shown in Figure 2.3 is for you to realize that there are many topics beyond cybersecurity that you also need to know in order to be a good cybersecurity professional. Many professionals have difficulty going deeper into cybersecurity because they lack basic knowledge of computer networks and operating systems. That's why it is critical that you build a good foundation before trying to learn about advanced topics. For example, after reading the *Rapid7's impact by OpenSSL Buffer Overflow Vulnerability* blog post, a user asks what a buffer overflow is. How can you give a confident answer if you don't know how an operating system works?

 Note

See the *Rapid7's impact by OpenSSL Buffer Overflow Vulnerability* blog post at *https://www.rapid7.com/blog/post/2022/11/11/rapid7s-impact-from-openssl-buffer-overflow-vulnerabilities-cve-2022-3786-cve-2022-3602/*.

 TIP

You can learn more about buffer overflow at *https://www.imperva.com/learn/application-security/buffer-overflow/*.

In this self-assessment phase, you can repeat the process above many times to identify your knowledge gaps. This should be a fun exercise because you will learn more about current attacks, and it will push you to understand your limits. Make sure to follow this process for at least one week before creating your learning plan.

TIP

Subscribe to free newsletters tailored to IT professionals that contain cyber-security topics. This will provide a smoother transition between reading topics you are familiar with and new topics requiring you to research more. For example, subscribe to the CompTIA Newsletter distributed by SmartBrief at *https://corp.smartbrief.com/advertise?_industry_advertise=tech.*

Create Your Plan

Before establishing a good plan, you should have a precise goal for this plan. Believe it or not, many people create a plan without even knowing their goal, which is why the plan often does not lead to successful execution.

In my book *Ready, Set, Achieve!: A Guide to Taking Charge of Your Life, Creating Balance, and Achieving Your Goals* —coauthored by Jodi Miller—I emphasize how the use of SMART Goals changed my life and enabled me to better plan my steps to achieve my personal and professional goals. Figure 2.4 shows what SMART means in this context.

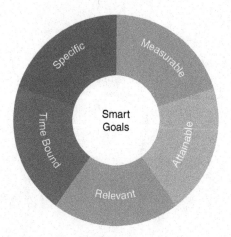

Figure 2.4 *SMART Goals*

 Note

You can learn more about this book at *https://www.amazon.com/Ready-Set-Achieve-Creating-Achieving-ebook/dp/B011AQDYOQ.*

By establishing your goals using this approach, you will clearly understand your direction and how you are progressing toward achieving your goal. Table 2.1 outlines how the SMART approach can be used.

Table 2.1 Using SMART Goals

Item	Definition	Example
Specific	Be very specific with your goal. Goals are often not accomplished because they are too broad and blurry.	After finishing my self-assessment, I noticed that I had a lot of gaps in operating system architecture. I want to learn about Linux operating systems and obtain a Linux certification.
Measurable	How will you measure whether the goal was accomplished?	Once I learn about operating systems, I will write a blog post about buffer overflow and share it with more experienced professionals so they can provide feedback.
Attainable	What is the point of setting an unrealistic goal? Don't mistake a goal for a vision. A vision usually is something that seems unrealistic because it is something that will likely take years to accomplish. Between now and achieving the vision, there will be multiple goals to accomplish. Therefore, a goal must be attainable in a feasible amount of time.	I want to learn more about operating systems to understand terms such as buffer overflow and memory leak.
Relevant	What is the relevance of this task to your overall goal? How can you focus on something that will impact your final goal?	I want to start sharing articles on LinkedIn about operating systems architecture and potential attacks. This will allow me to interact with other professionals with more knowledge to share about this subject.
Time-bound	When are you planning to achieve this goal? This is probably one of the most important elements of SMART goals because a goal without a deadline is just a wish. Make sure to establish a precise timeline for your goal.	I want to accomplish this goal in three months.

The example shown in Table 2.1 gives you an idea of how SMART Goals can help you in the journey to achieve goals. Most likely, you will have to do this exercise multiple times in your career, and it will become easier to correlate your ideas with the appropriate themes every time you do.

Organizing Your Plan

Having a clear plan is essential for your success, and as part of this plan, you will need to establish a series of tasks that will lead you closer each day to achieving your final goal. For this reason, you must organize your plan in such a way that you can track things that were done and need to be done.

Although there are many tools in the market for that, I like simplicity, and in my opinion, Microsoft Planner is a simple way to organize your plans and track your progress. With Microsoft Planner, you can create a plan; within it, you can establish many parameters, as shown in Figure 2.5.

Figure 2.5 *New plan in Microsoft Planner*

 Note

Watch this Microsoft Planner tutorial for more information: *https://youtu.be/ LIH2K-Vt3dl.*

Figure 2.5 shows the main fields for creating a new plan using Microsoft Planner. You can track your progress and create a checklist of activities. In this example, my timeline is four months. Each item on the checklist is a phase that can take multiple weeks. My overall plan in Microsoft Planner is shown in Figure 2.6.

Figure 2.6 *Overall plan in Microsoft Planner*

Now that I have this broad view of my plan, I can start being more specific with each phase. As you can see in Figure 2.6, you have the option to add an item to your backlog. If you have already started Phase 1, then you should create a new task in the In Progress column. Figure 2.7 shows an example of the Phase 1 details:

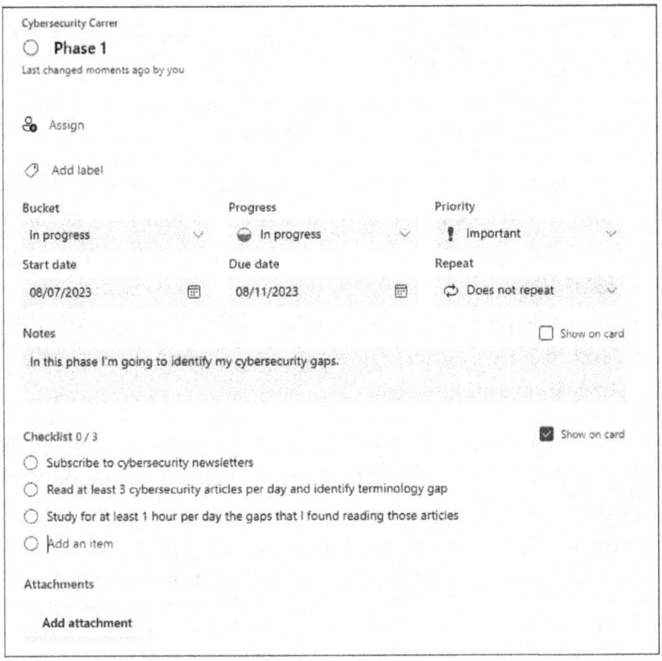

Figure 2.7 *Task created for Phase 1*

Notice that in this task, you established a more granular checklist tailored for this phase. As you go through each one of the checklist items, you can mark them as complete. Now, you need to add Phase 2 in the Up Next column and Phases 3 to 5 in the Backlog column.

 TIP

> By the end of this book, you should have enough material to create all the tasks for Phases 2 to 5. Take notes as you go through the chapters for items specific to your needs. While the material in this book will allow you to create a core plan, many items within tasks will be very particular to your own needs.

Cybersecurity Certifications

There are many cybersecurity certifications available—some with more industry recognition than others—but before even looking at certifications, it is important to understand the value that a certification gives to you from a learning perspective. I'm a big believer in and advocate of industry certifications because they give you a learning roadmap for a particular domain. Even if you believe certifications will not give you an advantage when trying to find a job—debatable because some jobs will explicitly ask for certain certifications—the point is that you will learn about the technology covered on the exam as you study for it.

If you study to prepare for a certification exam, that knowledge is yours, regardless of the title. You need to focus on that because it's all about the journey, not the destination. I always tell my mentees and students that while it is important to reach the desired destination, what builds your knowledge and character is the journey you go through while prepping for the exam. The hours you invested in building labs, testing, and reading chapters are yours, even if your employer doesn't care about the certification you just earned.

Just like anything else in life, it is about perspective, and once you change your perspective about the direct gain you will achieve by studying for a certification, you will see the true value of being a certified professional. Now, this assumes that you don't use cheating methods like braindumps or things of this nature. Using these methods is a waste of your time and money and unethical. Don't do it!

1:1 WITH THE AUTHOR: CERTIFICATION VERSUS COLLEGE DEGREES

As a university professor for many years, the most common question I get is whether getting a certification or a degree in cybersecurity is better.

My answer is always, "It depends." Ideally, you should have both, but if you have to choose one to start, you need to understand your immediate goal. If you are looking for a job requiring specific certifications, then go after those certifications. If you are looking for long-term gain and the possibility of aiming for higher jobs that require higher education, then go for a formal degree (Master's or Ph.D. in cybersecurity). It all depends on your goal and your current conditions.

I started my IT Career in 1994, and in 1997, I obtained my first IT Certification—MCP (Microsoft Certified Professional)—after passing the Windows 95 Exam. I needed this certification because my employer needed two MCPs in the company to become a Microsoft Authorized Training Center, and I was one of the two selected to get it. In other words, at that time, it was a business need that aligned with my career aspirations.

Since 1994, I've gotten some certifications based on business needs and others because I wanted to learn about a subject, and the certification gave me the roadmap for that. Regarding security certification, my first one was CompTIA Security+, which I obtained in 2005. At the time, I was working on more security-related topics, and I decided to invest in CompTIA Security+ because I saw the opportunity to improve my foundational knowledge of security.

As a manager, when I'm looking at resumes to select interview candidates, I have different approaches to triage, which vary according to the position I'm opening. If the position I'm opening requires an experienced professional who can join the team and "hit the ground running" with little ramp-up time, then I will prioritize experience. Sometimes, I find many candidates with similar experiences, so I look at other factors like formal education and certifications. However, if it is an entry-level position, and most of the candidates don't have experience in cybersecurity, the certification will have even more value to me because at least shows that the candidate is doing their homework by studying, learning, and getting certified. In other words, when comparing two entry-level candidates without cybersecurity experience, I'll likely select one with security certifications for the interview loop.

Investing in certifications is never a waste of time and money because if you are studying for an exam, you are learning the subject, and that knowledge is yours. Nobody can take that away from you. In addition, if you are investing in a cybersecurity degree while already certified, you are covering all your bases. This enriches your resume and gives you even more knowledge.

Because many certifications are available, I cover the main ones according to the job function and specialization. But let's first set the stage with some foundational security certifications.

Foundational Security Certifications

I am often asked: "If I want to work with cybersecurity, what is the very first certification I should take?" Here we go with my favorite answer: it depends. While this answer annoys many people, I always ask follow-up questions about the person's background. Each person has a different need, so giving a standard answer to everyone doesn't seem to be the best approach to me. Doing so would be like putting everyone who wants to lose weight on the same diet. They won't get the same result.

Having said that, let's review some of the main certifications that can give you the knowledge you need to get started.

 Important

The order below does not reflect the certifications that are more important or have a better reputation.

Cybersecurity Fundamentals by ISACA

This is a great certification to get started, and it is offered by a very well-known organization with more than 50 years in the market—the Information Systems Auditing & Control Association (ISACA). This certification covers four domains:

- Securing assets (35 percent of the exam)
- Information security fundamentals (27 percent of the exam)
- Security operations and response (20 percent of the exam)
- Threat landscape (18 percent of the exam)

 Note

As you can see, this is a very complete body of content covering all the major principles. To learn more about this certification, visit *https://www. isaca.org/credentialing/itca/cybersecurity-fundamentals-certificate.*

Certified in Cybersecurity (CC) by ISC2

This is a relatively new certification focused on cybersecurity fundamentals. The biggest advantage of this certification is the vendor—the International Information System Security Certification Consortium (ISC2). ISC2 is a reputable organization and very well respected across the entire cybersecurity industry.

The main ISC2 certification is CISSP, and that's the one many cybersecurity professionals know ISC2 for. However, ISC2 felt the market needed an entry-level cybersecurity certification, so they created the CC. This certification covers five domains:

- Security principals (26 percent of the exam)

- Network Security (24 percent of the exam)

- Access Controls Concepts (22 percent of the exam)

- Security Operations (18 percent of the exam)

- Business Continuity, Disaster Recovery, and Incident Response (10 percent of the exam)

 Note

To learn more about this certification, visit *https://www.isc2.org/ Certifications/CC.*

Cyber and IT Security Foundation by Exin

Exin was founded in 1984 and, over the years, has been recognized as one of the leading certification organizations, with more than 3 million certified professionals in different fields worldwide. The Cyber and IT Security Foundation certification is part of the Exin Foundation–level program. This certification covers the following topics (no percentage is assigned to each topic):

- TCP/IP networking

- Computer systems

- Applications and databases

- Cryptography

- Identity and access management

- Cloud computing

- Exploiting vulnerabilities

One of the things I really like about this certification is that it covers core TCP/IP networking concepts. In my opinion, this is a differentiator factor when it comes to foundational knowledge. I would even say this could be your first certification as you transition from a different field to cybersecurity. I've seen some students take this certification first, followed by the ISC2 CC. In other words, you can have two certifications to further solidify your foundational knowledge. As I always say, each person has a different need. Build your plan according to your needs.

 Note

For more information about this certification, visit *https://www. exin.com/data-protection-security/exin-cyber-and-it-security/ exin-cyber-and-it-security-foundation/*.

Security+ by CompTIA

The Computing Technology Industry Association (CompTIA) is a vendor-neutral, independent source of information on a wide range of technology topics.

CompTIA certifications are well recognized in the market, and Security+ certification is well-aligned with the National Initiative for Cybersecurity Education (NICE) framework. NICE is sponsored by the National Institute of Standards and Technology (NIST) in partnership with academia and the private sector. Security+ certification covers the following topics:

- Attacks, threats, and vulnerabilities (24 percent of the exam)
- Architecture and design (21 percent of the exam)
- Implementation (25 percent of the exam)
- Operations and incident response (16 percent of the exam)
- Governance, risk, and compliance (14 percent of the exam)

As I mentioned, Security+ was my first security certification, and I learned a lot from it. I also wrote an entire prep guidebook for the Security+ certification released in Portuguese (the first book about this certification ever to be released in Brazil) and trained hundreds of professionals over the years to help them pass the exam (during the 401 version of the exam). Because of this certification's impact on many careers, Security+ will always be one of the main certifications I recommend for beginners.

Note

For more information about this certification, see *https://www.comptia.org/certifications/security.*

Certified Security Specialist (ECSS) by EC-Council

EC-Council is a global information security education, training, and certification leader. The EC-Council's most well-known certification is the Certified Ethical Hacker (CEH), which is way more advanced. This certification covers the following topics:

- Information security and networking fundamentals (9 percent of the exam)
- Information security threats and attacks (21 percent of the exam)
- Information security controls (23 percent of the exam)
- Wireless network, VPN, and web application security (17 percent of the exam)
- Ethical hacking and pen testing (1 percent of the exam)
- Incident response and computer forensics fundamentals (6 percent of the exam)
- Digital evidence and file systems (4 percent of the exam)
- Windows and network forensics (10 percent of the exam)
- Logs and email crime forensics (6 percent of the exam)
- Investigation report (3 percent of the exam)

This is another example of a very granular body of content covering many aspects of cybersecurity, including areas not covered by any other exam, such as forensics and ethical hacking. The advantage of such broad exposure is that you may relate to some of these fields of expertise and pursue more specialized certifications.

Note

For more information about this certification, see https://www.eccouncil.org/programs/certified-security-specialist-ecss/.

TIP

All these certifications have network infrastructure and operating system components in some way covered in the exam, hence the criticality that you have these skills as mentioned in Chapter 1.

Cybersecurity Analyst and Security Practitioners Certifications

Many professional certifications are designed for the cybersecurity analyst role and security practitioners. However, regardless of which one you pursue next, remember that you can't skip the foundational certifications unless you already have all the knowledge covered by them.

The following list has some of the main Cybersecurity Analyst certifications in the market. Keep in mind the intention here is not to give you the ultimate list of certifications. Instead, I am providing a list of certifications that I believe, based on my experience, can make a difference in your career. For example, these certifications could add critical knowledge for a particular role and give you the advantage of having an industry certification tailored for it.

Cybersecurity Analyst (CySA+) by CompTIA

One of the biggest advantages of this certification is that the exam includes hands-on questions. As you study for this certification, you will gain both a theoretical understanding of the technologies and hands-on knowledge of how to do some of the tasks.

If you are new to Cybersecurity and just finished the foundational track, you can start with this certification to gain hands-on practice in different scenarios based on real-world situations. This certification covers the following topics:

- Threat and vulnerability management (22 percent of the exam)
- Software and systems security (18 percent of the exam)
- Security operations and monitoring (25 percent of the exam)
- Incident response (22 percent of the exam)
- Compliance and assessment (13 percent of the exam)

Note

I became CySA+ certified during the beta phase of this exam, and I truly enjoyed the experience. I also released a dedicated CySA+ Exam prep book (at that time, it was called CSA+) in Portuguese. To obtain more information about this certification, visit *https://www.comptia.org/certifications/cybersecurity-analyst.*

Systems Security Certified Practitioner (SSCP) by ISC2

This is another great certification from ISC2, and it meets U.S. Department of Defense (DoD) Directive 8570.1. This certification is also good for IT professionals migrating to cybersecurity after acquiring the foundational skills. This certification covers the following topics:

- Access controls (15 percent of the exam)

- Security operations and administrator (16 percent of the exam)

- Risk identification, monitoring, and analysis (15 percent of the exam)

- Incident response and recovery (14 percent of the exam)

- Cryptography (9 percent of the exam)

- Network and communication security (16 percent of the exam)

- Systems and application security (15 percent of the exam)

 Note

Read more about U.S. Department of Defense (DoD) Directive 8570.1 at *https://www.isc2.org/Training/US-Government.*

 TIP

As you can see, this certification has a more granular approach regarding the distribution of topics covered on the exam. To learn more about this certification, visit *https://www.isc2.org/Certifications/SSCP.*

Certified Cybersecurity Technician (CICT) by EC-Council

This certification focuses on hands-on skills and requires you to learn how to read logs to identify malicious activity, which you can only do if you have hands-on practice.

This type of certification is a great alternative for professionals working in a job that doesn't expose them to these technologies and scenarios. In other words, you will learn things you won't be able to learn in your current job because you don't work in cybersecurity yet. The page for this certification doesn't specify the percentage of the topics covered in the exam, but it provides the topics covered by the course.

 Note

> For more information, visit *https://www.eccouncil.org/programs/certified-cybersecurity-technician-certification*.

Specializations

You can easily go off the rails regarding cybersecurity certifications. Covering every certification in detail would require a dedicated chapter for each vendor, which is unnecessary since all the information is available on the vendor's website. Instead, this section lists the main specialized certifications from the primary industry vendors.

Table 2.2 maps the main certifications according to the professional field of specialization.

Table 2.2   Specializations

Field	Certification	Vendor
Professionals who work on the red team (pen testers and related jobs)	Pentest+	CompTIA
	GIAC Penetration Tester (GPEN)	GIAC
	CIPENT	EC-Council
	GIAC Exploit Researcher and Advanced Penetration Tester (GXPN)	GIAC
	GIAC Certified Incident Handler (GCIH)	GIAC
	OSCP	Offensive Security
	EICIH	EC-Council
	EICEH	EC-Council
Professionals who work with cloud security	CICSE	EC-Council
	GIAC Cloud Security Essentials (GCLD)	GIAC
	GIAC Cloud Threat Detection (GCTD)	GIAC
	CCSP	ISC2

Field	Certification	Vendor
Digital forensics	CIHFI	EC-Council
	GIAC Certified Forensic Examiner (GCFE)	GIAC
	GIAC Battlefield Forensics and Acquisition (GBFA)	GIAC
Cybersecurity architects	CISSP (see table footnote)	ISC
	CASP	CompTIA
Security managers and leaders	GIAC Security Leadership (GSLC)	GIAC
	GIAC Strategic Planning, Policy, and Leadership (GSTRT)	GIAC
	GIAC Security Operations Manager (GSOM)	GIAC
	Certified CISO	EC-Council
	EXIN Information Security Officer	EXIN

CISSP can also be required in some security manager positions. Because the scope of this certification is so broad, it also often fits in security leadership roles.

Vendor-Specific Certifications

So far, all the certifications covered in this chapter are technology agnostic. In other words, they aren't specific to Microsoft, Google, Amazon, Cisco, or any software or hardware company that owns the certification. This agnostic approach is good because it prepares you for a broader range of technologies. The information you learn can apply to many platforms. However, as you start looking for jobs, you might realize that some companies require you to be certified in a specific technology. For example, you may find a job where the hiring manager requires the applicant to be a Microsoft Certified Cybersecurity Architect because this job is focused on Microsoft security technologies.

This becomes even more common in the cloud computing environment, where three main cloud providers (Amazon, Microsoft, and Google) have their own certification tracks. The certification track established by each cloud provider focuses on its own technology and how to plan, design, and implement aspects particular to its cloud platform. Table 2.3 shows the primary exams/certifications for Amazon, Microsoft, and Google that are relevant for cybersecurity professionals.

Table 2.3   Cloud provider security certifications

Provider	Certification/Exam
Microsoft	
	Microsoft Azure Security Technologies (AZ-500)
	Microsoft Security Operations Analyst (SC-200)
	Microsoft Cybersecurity Architect (SC-100)
	Microsoft Security, Compliance, and Identity Fundamentals (SC-900)
Google	Professional Cloud Security Engineer
Amazon	AWS Certified Security

 TIP

When it comes to cloud provider certifications, it is important that you also have the foundational knowledge of each provider. Each cloud provider has its own series of foundational exams. For example, Azure has its Exam AZ-900: Microsoft Azure Fundamentals.

Summary

In this chapter, you learned how to self-assess the gaps in your cybersecurity knowledge. You learned the importance of using SMART Goals to achieve your goals, how to create a plan, and most importantly, how to organize this plan in such a way that you can track progress. Lastly, you learned about the role of cybersecurity certifications in your career from an employment and learning perspective. In the next chapter, you will learn how to create your own lab in the cloud and how to use it to continue sharpening your skills.

3

Building Your Lab

"Knowledge is of no value unless you put it into practice."

–Anton Chekhov

Now you know what you want. You have identified the cybersecurity area you want to work in, identified your current gaps, and established a plan. As part of this plan, you should have added time to ramp up with the technology areas in which you need to improve.

However, you can read about these technologies all day long, but if you don't do hands-on practice, your knowledge will be limited, which might affect you while interviewing. When you don't have hands-on experience in a subject, it's hard to feel confident that you can actually implement the things you just learned about in theory.

With the number of online resources we have nowadays, it's easier to create your own lab to implement scenarios that will help you gain more experience. This chapter will assist you in creating a lab and suggest some scenarios you can use to put things into practice.

Lab Requirements

While different cybersecurity jobs will require different skills, the goal here is to ensure that you have a good foundational understanding of technologies that can be utilized across different cybersecurity job roles. Building this foundational lab allows you to continue adding new scenarios to learn different skills.

To create this foundational lab, you need to cover some core scenarios, and based on these scenarios, you will have the minimum requirements for this lab. Table 3.1 highlights what's covered in each of the scenarios in the lab I'm proposing:

Table 3.1 Lab scenarios and requirements

Scenario	Level	Minimum requirements
Understand operating system processes and threads	Basic (100)	One virtual machine (VM) Windows operating system (OS) Process Monitor by Sysinternals
Understanding the communication between two hosts in the same TCP/IP subnet	Basic (100)	Two virtual machines (VMs) Windows OS Wireshark
Cloud security posture management	Intermediate (200)	Azure subscription Microsoft Defender for Cloud

Scenario	Level	Minimum requirements
Multicloud security posture management	Intermediate (200)	Azure subscription AWS account GCP project Microsoft Defender for Cloud
Understanding regulatory and compliance standards	Intermediate (200)	Azure subscription Microsoft Defender for Cloud
Simulating and detecting attacks on Windows and Linux	Advanced (300)	Azure subscription Linux OS Microsoft Defender for Servers Four virtual machines (VMs) Windows OS
Implementing a cloud-based security information and event management (SIEM)	Advanced (300)	Azure subscription Microsoft Sentinel
Threat hunting	Advanced (300)	Azure subscription Microsoft Defender for Cloud Microsoft Sentinel
Gathering threat intelligence	Advanced (300)	Azure subscription Microsoft Sentinel MITRE ATT&CK Framework

 Note

While you can use other tools for these scenarios, most enterprise-level security tools require a license, and trial versions of the Microsoft products shown in Table 3.1 are available. These allow you to learn without having to pay for the software. One alternative for an open-source lab is https://labs.fedoraproject.org/en/security/.

One important thing to mention about Table 3.1 is that the suggested minimum requirements are based on the material I cover in this chapter. However, nothing stops you from adding other elements to this scenario. For example, in implementing a cloud-based security information and event management (SIEM) scenario, the minimum requirement is to use a Microsoft SIEM solution called Microsoft Sentinel. However, you can build your own lab to use another solution, such as Splunk.

While thinking about potential additions to each scenario, consider whether those additions will cost money. My intent is to help you build a free lab to practice. Remember that once you start deploying these solutions, your clock starts, and you need to finish everything in a specific time frame since some of these solutions are free only during a trial period. That's why it is so important to clearly define everything you want to test and practice during this ramp-up phase. Figure 3.1 has an example of how you can plan your trial usage, assuming a 30-day trial (which is the case for most of the products used in this lab):

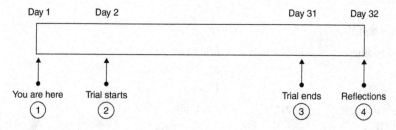

Figure 3.1 *Roadmap to conclude the lab*

The diagram shown in Figure 3.1 has four major phases:

- **You are here:** This is where you are right now, reading this chapter and defining which scenarios you want to implement. For example, if you are already an IT professional migrating to cybersecurity, you might not need to implement scenarios 1 and 2.

- **Trial starts:** Once you have enumerated which scenarios you want to implement, then you can start deploying the products, which usually entails starting the trial period for that product and also for the platform (in this case, Azure).

- **Trial ends:** Add the ending date on your calendar, and add a calendar reminder at least 10 days before the trial expires. Some of these products will require you to supply a credit card number when you sign up for a trial. While they don't charge you upfront if you go over the 30 days, they will start charging for the next cycle. So, make sure to cancel your subscription before the 30th day of use. This 10-day reminder prompts you to evaluate what you have done so far and whether anything is missing. If you've already implemented all scenarios and are ready to move on, just cancel the subscription.

- **Reflections:** After everything is done, you should pause for a day and reflect on the lessons learned. A good way to practice what you've learned is to write a report with your observations about each scenario. This report should contain more than just copy-and-pasted material from articles you read to help you with the lab. Instead, it should include your thoughts about what you have learned and whether you believe there are still some areas you need to continue improving as you move forward. This report will also help you to prioritize the areas you need to improve and the areas where you already feel confident.

The following sections will go over each scenario. Some scenarios will have less-detailed explanations because they're already very well documented on the websites I reference in this chapter.

Creating Your Lab

The first step to creating your own lab is to select the cloud platform you will use to deploy your lab. This chapter will use the Azure platform to deploy the lab. However, for scenarios one and two, you can use your personal computer to perform the required tasks. Here are a couple of things to remember when reading these scenarios:

- If you already have experience performing the tasks for scenarios one and two, you can skip to scenario three.

- The explanation provided in this chapter won't go into deep technical details about each element covered in the scenarios. The intent here is for you to gain familiarity with the terminologies, gain some hands-on experience, and use it as a foundation to get started. You must be diligent and look for other sources of information regarding the technologies covered in each scenario. Some resources tailored to each scenario are available at *yuridiogenes.us*.

Scenario 1—Operating Systems Process

A deep understanding of operating systems is critical for any cybersecurity professional. You can access a curated list of online resources and books I recommend to learn more about operating systems by visiting *yuridiogenes.us*. There, you will find a section dedicated to this book where you can see the references per chapter.

For this first scenario, you can use your own computer if you have Windows 10 or 11 installed. Once you confirm the Windows version, follow these steps:

1. Download Process Monitor from the Systeinternals website and store it in a folder named **Temp** on the C: drive. (If you don't already have a Temp folder, create it and extract the files there.)

2. Before launching **Procmon.exe**, make sure to close all open applications.

3. Once you do that, double-click **Procmon.exe**.

4. On the **Process Monitor License Agreement** page, click **Agree**.

5. If the **User Account Control** window pops up, click **Yes**, and you should see a dashboard like the one shown in Figure 3.2.

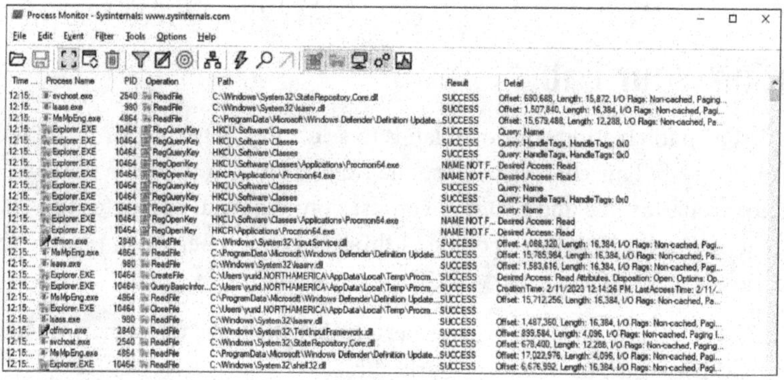

Figure 3.2 *Process Monitor*

This dashboard can be overwhelming at first, but you need to understand why you are here in the first place. When a program is executed, a process is created. Each process has a name, which is represented in the **Process Name** column in the **Process Monitor** dashboard. Each process receives a unique identifier (ID) shown in the **PID** column. (PID means process ID.)

Figure 3.2 shows an example of the Explorer.exe process, which appears multiple times, meaning multiple operations are happening. The operation's name that appears in the **Operation** column might be the same, but the path may vary. For example, the Explorer.EXE process may be querying multiple registry keys. The **Result** column is important because it shows the result of the operation done by the process in the path shown in the **Path** column. To better understand this, do a simple test:

1. In the **Process Monitor**, click **Filter** and then click the **Filter** option.

2. Select **Process Name**.

3. In the name field, type **notepad.exe** and click the **Add** button.

4. Click the **OK** button.

5. Once the filtering is finished, click the Windows Start icon, type **notepad.exe**, and press **Enter**.

6. Now review the number of things that happened just by executing notepad.exe.

7. The **Process Monitor** window will be empty, and after you execute the previous step, you will notice the process and a thread being created, as shown in Figure 3.3.

Time ...	Process Name	PID	Operation	Path	Result	Detail
3:24:2...	notepad.exe	10648	Process Start		SUCCESS	Parent PID: 10464, Command line: "C:\WINDO...
3:24:2...	notepad.exe	10648	Thread Create		SUCCESS	Thread ID: 9416
3:24:2...	notepad.exe	10648	CreateFile	C:\Windows\System32\notepad.exe	SUCCESS	Desired Access: Generic Read, Disposition: Ope...
3:24:2...	notepad.exe	10648	QueryStandardI...	C:\Windows\System32\notepad.exe	SUCCESS	AllocationSize: 204,800, EndOfFile: 201,216, Nu...
3:24:2...	notepad.exe	10648	QueryDeviceInf...	C:\Windows\System32\notepad.exe	SUCCESS	Device Type: Disk, Characteristics: Secure Open
3:24:2...	notepad.exe	10648	QueryEAFile	C:\Windows\System32\notepad.exe	SUCCESS	
3:24:2...	notepad.exe	10648	QueryEAFile	C:\Windows\System32\notepad.exe	SUCCESS	
3:24:2...	notepad.exe	10648	QueryStreamInf...	C:\Windows\System32\notepad.exe	SUCCESS	0: ::$DATA
3:24:2...	notepad.exe	10648	CloseFile	C:\Windows\System32\notepad.exe	SUCCESS	
3:24:2...	notepad.exe	10648	Load Image	C:\Windows\System32\notepad.exe	SUCCESS	Image Base: 0x7ff7f91f0000, Image Size: 0x38000
3:24:2...	notepad.exe	10648	CreateFile	C:\Windows\System32\ntdll.dll	SUCCESS	Desired Access: Generic Read, Disposition: Ope...
3:24:2...	notepad.exe	10648	QueryStandardI...	C:\Windows\System32\ntdll.dll	SUCCESS	AllocationSize: 2,031,616, EndOfFile: 2,028,984, ...
3:24:2...	notepad.exe	10648	QueryDeviceInf...	C:\Windows\System32\ntdll.dll	SUCCESS	Device Type: Disk, Characteristics: Secure Open
3:24:2...	notepad.exe	10648	QueryEAFile	C:\Windows\System32\ntdll.dll	SUCCESS	
3:24:2...	notepad.exe	10648	QueryStreamInf...	C:\Windows\System32\ntdll.dll	SUCCESS	0: ::$DATA
3:24:2...	notepad.exe	10648	CloseFile	C:\Windows\System32\ntdll.dll	SUCCESS	
3:24:2...	notepad.exe	10648	Load Image	C:\Windows\System32\ntdll.dll	SUCCESS	Image Base: 0x7ff95e390000, Image Size: 0x1f8...
3:24:2...	notepad.exe	10648	CreateFile	C:\Windows\Prefetch\NOTEPAD.EXE-...	SUCCESS	Desired Access: Generic Read, Disposition: Ope...
3:24:2...	notepad.exe	10648	QueryEAFile	C:\Windows\Prefetch\NOTEPAD.EXE-...	SUCCESS	

Figure 3.3 *Events generated by executing notepad.exe*

A process can create one or more threads, the basic unit the OS will use to allocate processor time. Why should you care about this information? Because when you are investigating a computer that is apparently compromised, you will use tools like Process Monitor to identify suspicious activities performed by a potentially malicious process.

 Tip

Before moving to scenario 2, perform some extra tests. For example, in the **Process Monitor**, create a filter for excel.exe, open Microsoft Excel, type some formulas, and save the file in the c:\temp folder. Now go to the **Process Monitor** and try to find the exact moment the file was saved. Right-click each operation and open its **Properties** to explore available information.

 Note

You can learn more about processes and threads at *https://bit.ly/cybercareerch3link2*.

 Note

Read this blog post to learn how Process Monitor can be used to investigate malicious activity: *https://bit.ly/cybercareerch3link3*.

Scenario 2—Network Traffic Analysis

Another foundational scenario you need to be familiar with is capturing and interpreting network traffic. Having a good understanding of how traffic flows between hosts is imperative for security professionals. While many tools are available to capture network traffic, the most common is Wireshark. This tool will enable your computer to listen to all network traffic and capture all frames for later analysis. Wireshark can also be used for network forensics and to identify malicious activities.

 Note

An example of network forensics with Wireshark can be found at *https://bit.ly/cybercareerch3link4*. An example of malicious traffic analysis using Wireshark can be found at *https://bit.ly/cybercareerch3link5*.

You can perform the steps below on your home computer, just like in scenario 1. To get started with this experiment, make sure to download and install Wireshark from *www.wireshark.org*. After that, follow the steps below:

1. Open Wireshark.

2. On the first screen, you should see the available network interfaces. For example, you will see multiple options if you have an Ethernet connection (cable) connected to your computer and a WiFi connection. For

this example, we will select **Ethernet**. (This option requires a cable connection to your computer.)

3. Right-click **Ethernet** and then click **Start Capture**.

4. At this point, you should see a lot of traffic on the screen.

5. Open your browser and go to *www.pearson.com*.

6. Go back to Wireshark, click the **Capture** menu, and then click **Stop**.

Now that you have captured the traffic, let's make some sense of it. In a TCP/IP network, when you try to access a domain by providing the domain name, such as *www.pearson.com*, the next step is to identify who owns that domain (in other words, identify the IP address). To do that, your local computer will consult the Domain Name Service (DNS) to resolve that name. Using Wireshark, you can create a filter to see exactly when this happened. Type **dns.qry.name == "www.pearson.com"** to filter DNS queries for *www.pearson.com*, as shown in Figure 3.4, and then press **Enter**.

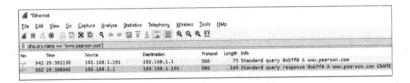

Figure 3.4 *Creating filters in Wireshark*

Notice that two packets appeared, one with the DNS query and the other with the DNS response. While the source and destination IP address from Figure 3.4 may vary according to your computer's network subnet, the point is that you were able to find exactly the moment that the name gets resolved. Now, let's see what a packet looks like. Click the first packet (DNS query), and you should see the different layers of information, as shown in Figure 3.5.

```
> Frame 942: 75 bytes on wire (600 bits), 7!
> Ethernet II, Src: HP_5e:0e:9e (a8:b1:3b:5e
> Internet Protocol Version 4, Src: 192.168.
> User Datagram Protocol, Src Port: 53968, [
> Domain Name System (query)
```

Figure 3.5 *Reading a network package*

These layers are explained below:

- The first layer on top contains information related to the frame itself.

- The second layer (Ethernet II) has the data-link layer, such as the computer's physical address, also known as Media Access Control (MAC) address. This address is unique for each network device.

- The third layer contains information about the network protocol in use, which in this case is the Internet Protocol (IP). Expanding this layer will show your computer's IP address and your DNS server's destination access.

- The fourth layer has information about the transport protocol in use, which, in this case, is the User Datagram Protocol (UDP). You will also find the source port (which will vary on each connection) and the destination port, which, in this case, is 53 (DNS service).

- The last layer contains information about the application, which, in this case, is DNS.

If you expand the transport and application layers, you should have a full visualization of the information you need for this exercise, as shown in Figure 3.6.

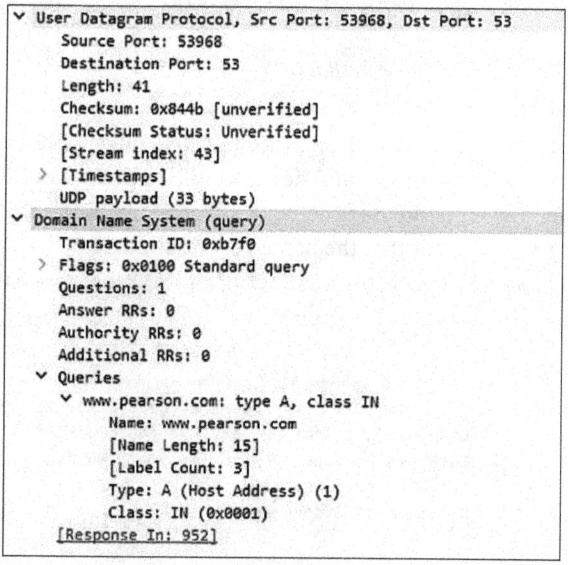

```
ˇ User Datagram Protocol, Src Port: 53968, Dst Port: 53
      Source Port: 53968
      Destination Port: 53
      Length: 41
      Checksum: 0x844b [unverified]
      [Checksum Status: Unverified]
      [Stream index: 43]
    > [Timestamps]
      UDP payload (33 bytes)
ˇ Domain Name System (query)
      Transaction ID: 0xb7f0
    > Flags: 0x0100 Standard query
      Questions: 1
      Answer RRs: 0
      Authority RRs: 0
      Additional RRs: 0
    ˇ Queries
        ˇ www.pearson.com: type A, class IN
            Name: www.pearson.com
            [Name Length: 15]
            [Label Count: 3]
            Type: A (Host Address) (1)
            Class: IN (0x0001)
      [Response In: 952]
```

Figure 3.6 *Analyzing a DNS query*

Repeat the same process for the second packet, the DNS response. In the response, you will see that the information is a bit different. Instead of having a section for queries, you will see a section for answers, as shown in Figure 3.7.

```
✓ Domain Name System (response)
    Transaction ID: 0xb7f0
  > Flags: 0x8180 Standard query response, No error
    Questions: 1
    Answer RRs: 3
    Authority RRs: 0
    Additional RRs: 0
  ✓ Queries
      ✓ www.pearson.com: type A, class IN
          Name: www.pearson.com
          [Name Length: 15]
          [Label Count: 3]
          Type: A (Host Address) (1)
          Class: IN (0x0001)
  ✓ Answers
      > www.pearson.com: type CNAME, class IN, cname wildcard.pearson.com.edgekey.net
      > wildcard.pearson.com.edgekey.net: type CNAME, class IN, cname e290.x.akamaiedge.net
      > e290.x.akamaiedge.net: type A, class IN, addr 173.222.216.14
    [Request In: 942]
    [Time: 0.007809000 seconds]
```

Figure 3.7 *Analyzing the DNS answer*

While this is a very simple analysis, it gives you an idea of the importance of understanding network traffic communication, protocols, and the use of Wireshark. New cybersecurity professionals who skip the foundational basics of computer networks have difficulty understanding how things work behind the scenes, impacting their capability to evolve in their field. For this reason, it is imperative to learn computer networks if you are going to work with cybersecurity.

 Tip

Before moving to scenario 3, perform some extra tests. For example, clear the DNS filter, type **SSL**, and analyze the SSL traffic. Review the Client Hello and Server Hello packets.

 Note

For more information about SSL handshake, see *https://bit.ly/ cybercareerch3link6.*

Scenario 3—Cloud Security Posture Management

If you plan to work in cybersecurity, you must learn about cloud computing. Once you learn about cloud computing, you will quickly understand why one of the challenges organizations face nowadays is ensuring they have visibility and control over all workloads provisioned in their cloud environment. In addition, most attacks against cloud workloads are successfully accomplished because of customer misconfiguration, mismanagement, and mistakes. You need a cloud security posture management (CSPM) solution to ensure your cloud environment is more secure.

 Note

Read this paper from NIST to learn the basics about Cloud Computing: *https://bit.ly/cybercareerch3link7*.

Microsoft Defender for Cloud is the CSPM solution we will use in this scenario. Since this is a very mature product, there are many resources available that you can use to ramp up on this technology. The team that I manage at Microsoft created a Defender for Cloud Public Lab to help customers to learn more about the product, so for this scenario, follow the steps below:

1. Visit *https://aka.ms/MDFCLabs*.

2. Perform the steps from the following modules:

    *   **Module 1:** In this module, you will provision your Azure environment using an Azure trial subscription.

    *   **Module 2:** In this module, you will learn more about Defender for Cloud and how it helps to manage the security posture of your cloud environment.

 Note

You can watch the *Defender for Cloud in the Field* show that I host to learn more about this product. Visit *https://aka.ms/MDFCInTheField* to watch all episodes.

After finishing these modules, you will have an environment ready for your 30 days trial. This means that now is the time to add the reminder on your calendar to ensure you cancel the subscription before the 30 days. Also, at this point, you must diligently perform all tests you need in this environment before the trial expires.

Scenario 4—Multi-Cloud Security

The "Flexera 2022 State of the Cloud Report" revealed that a multi-cloud approach is still the de facto standard among 89 percent of the organizations surveyed. This means you're very likely to find a job in the cybersecurity field that requires you to know the main cloud providers—Microsoft (Azure), Amazon (AWS), and Google (GPC). Security posture management across multiple cloud providers can be even more challenging, and that's why the CSPM solution must be able to provide visibility and control across clouds.

Defender for Cloud has this capability, and you can test it in the same lab environment that you started during scenario 3. To do that, go to *https://aka.ms/MDFCLabs* and complete modules 10 (GCP) and 11 (AWS). These modules will enable you to connect to each cloud provider and allow the information to flow to the Defender for Cloud dashboard.

 Note

Read the "Flexera 2022 State of the Cloud Report" at *https://bit.ly/cybercareerch3link9.*

Scenario 5—Regulatory Compliance

As you look for cybersecurity jobs, you must be mindful of the industry you will be working in. For example, if you are going to be a cybersecurity analyst in a hospital (health industry), you might need to know the regulatory standards required for that industry. You don't need to be an expert, but you should know what this means for the workloads you protect. Some of these workloads might need to comply with the Health Insurance Portability and Accountability Act (HIPAA).

The cloud security posture management platform needs to provide awareness of your workload's security state. It needs to also provide security recommendations to help improve those workloads' security posture by tailoring the hardening according to the industry standard, which, in this case, is HIPAA (Health Insurance Portability and Accountability Act of 1996).

To practice that, you will use the same lab from scenarios 3 and 4, but now you will follow the steps from Module 4.

Scenario 6—Attack Simulation

Many organizations adopt the red and blue teams strategy to better understand how threat actors operate and exploit vulnerabilities:

- **Red team**   The red team is responsible for constantly attacking its own platform to identify breaches before the threat actors do it.

- **Blue team**   The blue team is composed of defenders—cybersecurity professionals with relevant skills to ensure the environment is more secure. The blue team will also incorporate feedback from the red team to improve their security controls and reduce the likelihood of compromise.

If you are planning to work in this area within the cybersecurity field, this scenario is very important for you. Here are the labs you should perform to practice attack simulation:

- **Attack simulation for Windows**   Visit *http://bit.ly/cybercareerch-3link10* and follow the steps to execute attacks against a Windows system and see how Defender for Cloud detects those attacks. Notice that the attacker and target VMs can be provisioned in the same environment you created in scenario 3.

- **Attack simulation for Linux**   Visit *https://bit.ly/cybercareerch3link11* and follow the steps to execute attacks against a Linux system. You can also provision the Linux VM in the same environment you created in scenario 3.

Scenario 7—Security Information and Event Management

Cybersecurity professionals who work on security operations (SOC) teams need to be familiar with the use of security information and event management (SIEM) systems. The goal of a SIEM solution is to aggregate data coming from different data sources, correlate this data, and enable security teams to consume this data for different purposes, including security investigation, incident response, and threat hunting.

Microsoft Sentinel is a cloud-based SIEM platform that operates on top of Azure but can ingest data coming from other cloud providers or on-premises resources. To practice hands-on activities in Microsoft Sentinel, visit *https://aka.ms/MSSentinelLab* and execute the steps from the following modules:

- **Module 1:** In this module, you will provision Microsoft Sentinel. You should use the Azure subscription trial you started in scenario 3.

- **Module 2:** In this module, you will start collecting data from different services.

- **Module 3:** In this module, you will create analytics rules and incidents.

- **Module 4:** In this module, you will learn more about incident management.

This is a long lab, so reserve enough time to perform it and review the terminologies you are unfamiliar with by visiting Microsoft Sentinel documentation at *http://aka.ms/SentinelDocs*.

Scenario 8—Threat Hunting

Threat hunting is a relatively new discipline that usually belongs to the security operations (SOC) team. Threat hunters usually perform a proactive investigation to identify indications of compromise (IOC) or indication of attack (IOA).

If you plan to work in the Security Operations Team, learning how to perform threat hunting is important. This expands your reach and adds an extra skill to your portfolio. Follow the steps below to practice different approaches for threat hunting (use the same Azure subscription that you used in previous scenarios for both tasks below):

1. Visit *https://aka.ms/MSSentinelLab* and execute the steps from Module 5.

2. This module will go over the steps on how to perform threat hunting using Microsoft Sentinel capabilities.

3. After you finish this module, visit *https://bit.ly/cybercareerch3link14* and execute the steps from there. This article will go over the steps to perform threat hunting using Defender for Cloud.

 Note

Learn more about the different functions of a Security Operations Team at *https://bit.ly/cybercareerch3link12*. To learn the difference between IOC and IOA, visit *https://bit.ly/cybercareerch3link13*.

Scenario 9—Threat Intelligence

The use of threat intelligence has expanded over the years, and nowadays, most large organizations already understand that they must have this capability available. Threat intelligence gives context and actionable insights on attacks (active and old ones), as well as potential threats to the environment. This information is critical for decision-makers and security teams to use and be better prepared to deal with threat actors.

The MITRE ATT&CK® framework is "a curated knowledge base and model for cyber adversary behavior, reflecting the various phases of an adversary's attack life-cycle and the platforms they are known to target." You can leverage this knowledge base to better understand how adversaries operate, which can be beneficial in many scenarios, including when you need to enrich your threat intelligence. Follow the steps below to learn how to navigate through the MITRE ATT&CK framework:

1.   Visit the MITRE ATT&CK website at *https://attack.mitre.org*.

2.   Click the **Search** button and type **ipconfig**. Wait until the results appear. Click the **ipconfig, Software S0100** link.

3.   The **ipconfig** page supplies the details about this command, the mapping for the technique, and the groups (adversaries) used by this command. Notice that the technique in which this command is used is mapped to **System Network Configuration Discovery.**

4.   Click this technique (**T1016**) to see that this is a subtechnique from **Discovery**. This means that in the discovery phase, the adversary is still trying to understand the environment. In other words, the threat actor is still at the beginning of their mission.

5.   The MITRE ATT&CK framework is highly utilized in many products, including Microsoft Sentinel and Microsoft Defender for Cloud. To practice using threat intelligence in a SIEM platform, visit *https://aka. ms/MSSentinelLab* and complete the steps from Module 7.

 Note

The definition for MITRE ATT&CK above is from the *MITRE ATT&CK: Design and Philosophy* ebook, which can be downloaded at *https://bit.ly/ cybercareerch3link15*.

 Tip

Before considering this scenario completed, spend more time navigating *https://attack.mitre.org*. For example, search for **Cobalt Strike**. When you open the Cobalt Strike page, look for **System Network Configuration Discovery** and then read the description about how Cobalt Strike uses this subtechnique.

Self-Assessment

I know this chapter has a lot of information to digest, and you must be tired by now. But, if you think about it, you just had a major tour across different cybersecurity areas and the opportunity to practice many things and learn many new technologies.

Since this chapter was created using the 30-day Azure subscription, it is important for you to use at least 20 days to do all scenarios and have 9 days spare to review exercises that you have identified as needing more attention.

After you finish implementing all scenarios, reviewing all concepts, and taking notes, use Table 3.2 to perform a self-assessment per scenario. Notice that the entries in the **Completion** and **Observations** columns for scenarios 1 and 2 are only examples. The rest of the table is blank, so you can write your own observations.

Table 3.2 Self-assessment per scenario

Scenario	Completion	Observations
Understand operating system processes and threads	*100 percent*	I feel comfortable with this topic. Still need to dig more to understand threads, but I have a good idea of how things work.
Understanding the communication between two hosts in the same TCP/IP subnet	*90 percent*	I really liked this one. I feel like I can work all day long reading network packages. While I felt passionate about this topic, I still have a lot to learn because my background is not in computers. Need to do more computer network training.
Cloud Security Posture Management		
Multicloud Security Posture Management		
Understanding regulatory and compliance standards		
Simulating and detecting attacks on Windows and Linux		
Implementing a cloud-based Security information and event management (SIEM)		
Threat hunting		

Scenario	Completion	Observations
Gathering Threat Intelligence		
Understand operating system process and threads		
Understanding the communication between two hosts in the same TCP/IP subnet		

In Table 3.2, in the first two examples for the first two scenarios, the goal of the **Completion** column is to track how far you went on that scenario. Remember that while scenarios 1 and 2 are straightforward, others are more complex and will take longer. Ideally, you should finish everything, but you own your agenda, and if you don't have time to finish everything, the only requirement is to be honest with yourself and take notes to document your level of completion.

Another important column in this table is the **Observations**. The examples provided for scenarios 1 and 2 are some of the things that you can add. I advise you to write down which scenarios you were more excited and passionate about. This is when you will discover what triggers and motivates you and what you believe would be a good investment of your time to learn more. These nine scenarios cover different areas of cybersecurity, from the very basic level to the most advanced. Being exposed to all these tools and guided labs during the 30-day trial is an excellent way to identify which area you would like to work in the future.

1:1 WITH THE AUTHOR: BEING PASSIONATE IS AN IMPORTANT STEP FOR CAREER PROGRESS

Over the years, many professionals have reached out to me to ask how they could make progress in their careers. Some mistakenly assumed that because everyone was going one way, they also needed to go that direction. You can drive your career based on what is hot at the moment if that's what makes you happy.

Unfortunately, most people choose their direction based on money. I understand that being financially stable and well-compensated for your work is important, but it's not everything. You can earn a lot of money, but if you feel miserable at work, your life will be miserable. At some point, you will realize that the money was not worth it.

On June 12, 2005, during the Stanford University commencement address, Steve Jobs said: "The only way to be truly satisfied is to do what you believe is great work, and the only way to do great work is to love what you do. If you haven't found it yet, keep looking, and don't settle. As with all matters of the heart, you'll know when you find it. And like any great relationship, it just gets better and better as the years roll on. So keep looking, don't settle."

This quote from Steve Jobs is perfect! It summarizes everything when it comes to a career. I hope you are migrating to cybersecurity because you feel passionate about it. And if you are not passionate yet, maybe all the scenarios you performed during this lab will give you something to think about and explore further.

I've seen many professionals who rose to the top because they were extremely passionate about what they did. At the same time, I've seen professionals change careers because they were not happy where they were. I remember talking to a friend who became a Judo Sensei after decades in the IT field. He told me that IT, for him, was a career that he liked, but he was never passionate about it. He was always passionate about martial arts, Judo in particular. He said that once he changed his career, he took a financial downgrade and had to readjust all his finances to break even. However, he said he was never happier, and his life changed completely. He doesn't regret the change. As a matter of fact, his only regret is that he didn't make the change earlier. He is still earning less money, but as I said earlier in this chapter, money isn't everything.

In summary: while there are plenty of opportunities in the cybersecurity field, you still need to decide your area of focus. Choose wisely when selecting where you will invest more time. Don't be driven only by the financial aspects, particularly if you are changing careers, as this is a great opportunity to reset and start over. Find your "why" and be passionate. If you do those things, your career will change for the better.

Summary

This chapter taught you how to create your cybersecurity lab based on nine scenarios. You learned about operating systems processes and threads, basic network communication, cloud security posture management, multicloud security, regulatory compliance, attack simulation, SIEM, threat hunting, and threat intelligence. In the next chapter, you will learn the importance of networking in the cybersecurity field, how to stay connected with the community, and how to leverage LinkedIn.

4

Networking

"Networking is the number one unwritten rule of success in business."

–Sallie Krawcheck

As with any other career, knowledge and experience are two core pillars of success, but there is this third unwritten pillar that many people ignore or think they don't need because they already have enough experience: networking.

The reality is that even the most experienced professionals need to have good networking skills to continue growing in their careers—and most importantly—continue being exposed to new opportunities. When people say to me, "Yuri, you were lucky to lead this project." Well, it's not really lucky. As a matter of fact, success is never about luck. When you have a good network, you are exposed to different scenarios and opportunities, which means the likelihood that you will be exposed to a project that needs your skills is way higher. That's when we can say you were in the right place at the right time. But that isn't luck; your success only happened because you worked your way into that network and positioned yourself to be ready for the challenge. The keyword here is "ready." Many people wait until they see the opportunity to start getting ready, but by the time they feel ready for the challenge, the opportunity is gone. The bottom line is that you should always be ready.

This chapter will explore the importance of networking, which opportunities are available, and how to improve your networking in cybersecurity.

Networking in Cybersecurity

The cybersecurity community is very collaborative and open to new ideas, collaborations, and contributions. If you are transitioning from another field to cybersecurity, it is always important to start building new connections with other cybersecurity professionals. One great way to do that is by attending security conferences.

BSides is a security conference that is very open to all professionals and usually doesn't cost much (*www.securitybsides.com*) compared to large events like Black Hat. When this chapter was written, BSides was hosted in 208 cities across 60 countries, providing excellent presentations and training. For example, at BSides DFW 2022, training ranged from an introduction to Kali Linux to exploring wireless networks with Wireshark. Not only is this a great opportunity for you to learn, but it's also a great way to start creating your network.

 Note

To read some history about how BSides started, see *https://bit.ly/cyberca-reerch4link11*, and for more about BSides DFW 2022, see *http://bsidesdfw. com/2022spkr.*

While the world changed after COVID-19 and became more open to online events, the reality is that the in-person experience has more advantages when it comes to networking. When you go to in-person security conferences, you can meet people during coffee breaks, after-hours parties, and so on. With an online experience, you usually don't have this type of opportunity (though online conferences will save you some money). So, be sure to attend at least a couple of conferences annually. To balance your budget, you can go to a less expensive one in your city (local events) and a more expensive one outside of town. Following are some of the main in-person security conferences:

- Black Hat (*blackhat.com*)

- Defcon (*defcon.org*)

- RSA Conference (*www.rsaconference.com*)

- Hacker Halted (*www.hackerhalted.com*)

- Blue Hat (*www.microsoft.com/bluehat*)

If you are already ISC2 CISSP–certified, try to find a chapter near you to find activities you can engage in. There are lots of opportunities to contribute to your local chapter and meet cybersecurity professionals. These local chapters usually have monthly in-person meetings you can attend to expand your network and better understand what's happening in the local market.

The Information System Security Association International (*www.issa.org*) is another example of a cybersecurity community with local chapters you can join (requires an annual membership fee) and meet other cybersecurity professionals in your area. They also have a lot of resources online for members, including a monthly magazine with many articles and discussions about trends in the market.

Regarding the online community, you can visit many other places to stay connected and start meeting other cybersecurity professionals. SANS has many free online resources and workshops. Visit *www.sans.org/mlp/cybersecurity-training-community* to see and register for these opportunities. EC-Council University Cyber Talks is another online community that offers many free resources and enables you to meet other cybersecurity professionals.

 Note

I had the opportunity to present at SANS Cloud Security Summit 2020; you can see the online experience at *https://bit.ly/cybercareerch4link12*. You can watch one of my presentations at EC-Council University CyberTalks at *https://bit.ly/cybercareerch4link3*.

1:1 WITH THE AUTHOR: NEW CONTACTS THAT LEAD TO NEW OPPORTUNITIES

In 2014, my friend Erdal Ozkaya and I submitted a proposal to Hacker Halted in Atlanta (see Figure 4.1). A couple of months after we sent the proposal, we received an email informing us that our presentation was accepted. We presented a session about the adoption of bring your own device (BYOD) and related security concerns. It was an amazing experience!

Figure 4.1 *Erdal (left) and me with the certificate of appreciation*

After the session, I visited the expo to check out the booth to network and meet people. The EC-Council University Booth caught my attention because I had just finished my master's in cybersecurity that year. I asked about the program and whether there were teaching opportunities. The EC Council dean was very interested in my resume because I had previous experience teaching at universities and had a master's degree, so we exchanged business cards.

Six months later, the dean emailed to say they had an open teaching position in their undergraduate cybersecurity program. After an interview, I got the position and have been teaching at EC-Council University since 2015.

This is just a quick example of how beneficial it could be to participate in security conferences. When you are intentional—when you know what you want to get out of it—great things can happen. It's one thing to attend a conference because your boss asked you to go. It's another to attend with a purpose, using all the opportunities to network.

Even though the conference organization only paid for my hotel and meals, while I paid for the flight, I didn't think twice about it because I saw it as an opportunity to expand my network, present in a bigger venue, improve my brand, and make new connections. I saw it as an investment, and I'm glad I did because buying those plane tickets has already paid off.

In summary: When going to conferences, be intentional, make connections, visit booths, ask about products, how they work, and so on. In the cybersecurity field, staying curious and asking questions is important. You will start to see these conferences as an investment not only in readiness but also in professional growth through the expansion of your network.

Look Inward

When building your cybersecurity network, you must consider the different areas available. Doing so will save you time and allow you to have multiple pipelines open, which might provide leads for multiple opportunities. Figure 4.2 shows the different networking areas you should explore.

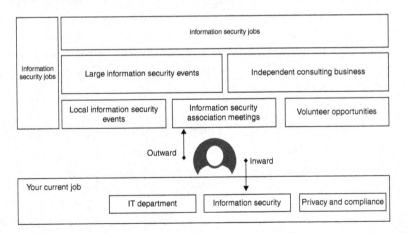

Figure 4.2 *Networking areas*

Figure 4.2 represents you at some point during your career transition. Job opportunities can come from different places, mainly when you are looking outward and engaging in activities that will expand your reach, knowledge, and network. Often, you must start small by visiting local security chapters in your city/area or a new area. However, never ignore the power of connections because these small chapters often bring opportunities for new security professionals where the perquisites are lower and more reachable given your current skills.

Another option for learning more about cybersecurity—and a great way to contribute to society—is volunteering. Many groups offer this type of opportunity, such as Hackers for Change. Volunteering allows you to learn and gain experience. Cybersecurity professionals usually have one thing in common: their purpose. Cybersecurity professionals understand their role in society and share a common goal of helping create a safer place for everyone. This common purpose drives the community to enable others to succeed because it's critical to have new professionals join the field.

 Note

For more information about Hackers for Change, see *https://www.hackersfor-change.com/volunteers*.

The reality is that your transition to cybersecurity will often happen as you continue to work in your current field. For example, if you are an IT professional working as a system administrator, you might not work directly with information security because another team manages that area. If that's the situation, you need to use the same networking principle to establish new connections and find opportunities inward. The only difference is that your network is composed of internal employees. Use the scenarios from Table 4.1, which assumes your current role is a system administrator, to learn how you can find opportunities to contribute and learn more about cybersecurity:

Table 4.1 Finding inward opportunities

Activity	Rationale	Tips to make it happen
Create a connection with your company's information security team	Building relationships with internal information security team members might open doors for future collaborations.	Research the internal distribution lists for internal teams and find out who the information security team members are. Schedule a 30-minute meeting with one of the members. In the invitation, introduce yourself and express the desire to learn more about security and see how you can partner with Information Security.

Activity	Rationale	Tips to make it happen
		When preparing for this meeting, make sure to have an organized agenda with the main topics you want to discuss. Remember, this meeting is not about you but how you can help and make yourself available to do some extra work that will allow you to contribute and learn.
Volunteer	Most organizations have more tasks than people, so there are always opportunities to volunteer to help.	Now that you have established the first contact, investigate how you can volunteer for information security work. Don't ignore low-level activities. For example, if they invite you to contribute with the information security documentation, show enthusiasm and get it done the best possible way. You want to ensure they see someone motivated and passionate about information security. The first impression they have from you in this first meeting is critical, so show passion about this topic and flexibility to adjust to their needs.
Find common projects	Now that you've done some volunteer work, it's time to see how you can make a more official partnership by participating in projects as a virtual team member (v-team).	When doing your volunteer work, be mindful of areas that you believe they (information security) could do differently. Use your current experience as a differentiating factor. Show the team that you bring value by using your unique vision as a system administrator. Bring ideas for improvement and share them with the information security team.

When you are changing careers—mainly when you are changing to a completely new field such as cybersecurity—you might see yourself constantly trying to catch up. You might overthink every situation and often get frustrated because you're unable to do cybersecurity work because your current job has nothing to do with security.

Overthinking can be your worst enemy and might completely sabotage your plan. During those difficult times, you need to go back to your plan and see if you are making progress. You often don't see progress until you go back to your original plan and accurately track your progress. That's why tools like Microsoft Planner, used in Chapter 2, can help you stay on track and avoid extra anxiety created by overthinking your lack of clarity on your progress.

Note

Some important tips about overthinking can be found at *https://bit.ly/ cybercareerch4link4.*

1:1 WITH THE AUTHOR: FINDING OPPORTUNITIES DURING CHALLENGING TIMES

In 2011, I worked as a technical writer for a team that created design consideration guides for private cloud security at Microsoft. The work was interesting, and the topic was very new then, so much research needed to be done. At the time, private cloud security was an alternative way for organizations still skeptical about public cloud security to adopt cloud technologies on their own datacenters.

In 2012, we had a reorganization at Microsoft, and I moved to the Windows Server networking team. This was frustrating because I didn't want to leave the security space, but I had no choice. I had invested heavily in security-related certifications and enjoyed working in that field.

After a couple of months in this role, I decided I couldn't rely only on my job to continue sharpening my cybersecurity skills. I needed to invest in something that could fill that gap, and that's when I decided to enroll in the Master of Cybersecurity program at UTICA College. I used the next two years (2012–2014) to continue learning more about the subject, expanding my outward network, and attending more conferences.

While doing my master's and working with the Windows network team, I started researching other teams doing more security-related work and inquiring how to partner and help. I did a lot of stretch assignments just to get involved. My friend Tom Shinder and I even created a talk show program called *From End to Edge and Beyond*, where we covered cybersecurity topics. In late 2012, we also released our book, *Windows Server 2012 Security from End to Edge and Beyond: Architecting, Designing, Planning, and Deploying Windows Server 2012 Security Solutions.* After the book was released, I partnered with other colleagues at Microsoft to write content and appeared as a guest writer for many blog posts. As you can see, my core work wasn't stopping me from investing time outside of my work hours to continue learning and creating security-related content. Later, Tom and I also created a talk show (at that time published by TechNet) called *From End to Edge and Beyond*, where we interviewed Microsoft security professionals.

In 2014, right after I finished my master's degree program and two years of investment in networking with other security teams within Microsoft, I moved to the enterprise mobility security team, where I started getting more specialized in BYOD security solutions. In 2015, I released my *Enterprise Mobility Suite Managing BYOD and Company-Owned Devices* book with my friend Jeff Gilbert. This book opened doors for me to speak at Microsoft Ignite and meet other security professionals.

In summary: If I had just crossed my arms when I felt frustrated and disappointed by being moved to a department I didn't want to work in, I probably would still be there. That's why it is always important to find opportunities even when the situation goes completely against your plans. Tough times will also bring unique opportunities, but you can only take advantage of those opportunities if you have an open mind and be flexible to adjust to the situation while moving forward. Remember that your plan is your north star, but you must be flexible to adjust along the way. Also, remember that you are a professional, which means your motivation should not influence the quality of your work. If you have goals to achieve in your career, do it, deliver with quality, and always protect your brand.

You can learn more about *Windows Server 2012 Security from End to Edge and Beyond: Architecting, Designing, Planning, and Deploying Windows Server 2012 Security Solutions* at *https://bit.ly/cybercareerch4link5*. You can see one of my guest appearances on the *Scripting Guy* blog at *https://bit.ly/cybercareerch4link6*.

Online Presence

Since the early 2000s, having a good online presence has been important, but as time passed, it became absolutely imperative to have a strong presence across the different platforms. As a cybersecurity professional, it's even more critical that your online presence is grounded in ethics and good standards.

As you create online profiles on different platforms, you need to understand the footprint you leave behind. Your social media presence can be tracked, allowing potential employers to see posts and comments you liked, posts you created, and even videos you watched on YouTube if you don't restrict your privacy and settings. If you already have a job and are engaging in social media discussion, always be mindful that your employer might be eligible to fire you because of things you say online. To avoid that, many professionals create two profiles: a personal profile that doesn't link to their real name and a professional profile that links to their real name. While this requires more maintenance, it really helps to isolate your different online footprints.

 Note

See this AskHR Q&A article for more about how your employer might react to what you do online: *https://bit.ly/cybercareerch4link8*.

LinkedIn

Using tools like LinkedIn has become a default part of the process to triage the massive amount of resumes received by recruiters and hiring managers. Recruiters and hiring managers often search LinkedIn for candidates' profiles to validate the information on their resumes. Some organizations are fully integrated on LinkedIn, meaning candidates can apply directly without uploading their resumes.

A survey from *The Manifest* revealed that 67 percent of companies use LinkedIn to hire people. Your online presence on professional social media like LinkedIn should be impeccable. When you apply for jobs, companies are likely to review your LinkedIn profile, and social media platforms like LinkedIn will help you connect with other professionals and expand your network.

 Note

You can read the entire survey from *The Manifest* at *https://bit.ly/ cybercareerch4link7*.

Joining a cybersecurity community group is a great way to connect with other people you don't know yet without sending a connection request. You can find all manner of groups by visiting *https://www.linkedin.com/search/results/groups*. If you want to narrow your filter to cybersecurity groups, type **#cybersecurity groups** in the search bar and press **Enter**. A sample result is shown in Figure 4.3.

You can navigate through the results, see which group looks more interesting, and then request to join. Upon joining the group, make sure to observe how the members behave regarding what they post, the type of comments, and the group's overall feel. Don't spam the group by sharing every article that you think is fascinating. Spend at least five days reconning the environment before you start engaging.

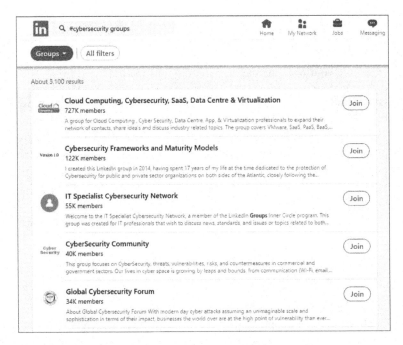

Figure 4.3 *Searching cybersecurity groups on LinkedIn*

 Tip

Before joining any group, make sure your LinkedIn profile is current with your current picture and relevant information about yourself, your education, and your job experience.

YouTube

If you are not paying close attention to the cybersecurity industry's overutilization of YouTube, you need to watch more closely. Cybersecurity professionals use You-Tube to disseminate information via free tutorials, online classes, and live webinars. If you are studying for the CompTIA Security+ certification, you can easily find free training on YouTube, including the famous Professor Messer channel (*youtube .com/@professormesser*), where he has many classes for CompTIA certifications.

While you should be leveraging YouTube for learning, you can also use it to expand your network. This can be done through many activities, including:

- Interacting with cybersecurity videos by leaving your comments and follow-up questions

- Subscribing to other cybersecurity professionals' channels

- Participating in live-streaming events and being active in the chat

- Creating your own channel and sharing information

You might think creating your own YouTube channel is a bit overwhelming, but it isn't. Just like you, many other professionals are trying to move to the cybersecurity field. At first, you might feel you have nothing to offer, but if you are already further along in your journey, you *do* have something to offer to the professionals who are still thinking about it. Ask yourself the following questions:

- What have I learned so far on this journey?

- Is there any lesson I believe would be interesting to share with other people?

- How could my personal struggles help motivate someone to keep moving forward?

- You might take these simple things for granted, but this is gold information for other people. If you look back on when you were still deciding what to do, you had a lot of uncertainties, too—just like many others have. So, consider creating your own YouTube channel and sharing your experiences in this field. Your videos can start very personal, almost like a journal. Still, with time, as you progress, you can start sharing technical tutorials to help people who are getting started. Later, when you're working daily in cybersecurity, you can start creating more advanced tutorials and sharing advanced experiences in the field. You don't have to wait until you've been in the field for three years to start contributing.

Twitter

Over the years, Twitter has become the center of many discussions, and cybersecurity is certainly one of those. From security researchers to specialized cybersecurity companies, they all use Twitter to bring awareness about cybersecurity-related issues. A simple Twitter search for the **#cybersecurity** hashtag can bring up a lot of Twitter accounts that you might want to follow to learn more about what's news in this field (see Figure 4-4).

You can use Twitter to learn more about the industry by following cybersecurity-related accounts, and you can also use it to start sharing information and building your brand. When used properly, Twitter can be a great tool because you can interact more actively with other users. While expanding your network is a good thing, don't get sidetracked with unrelated conversations that deviate from your main goal because it is also very easy to start incorporating Twitter's vibe of the day into your personal life and derail into a rant mode about something going on in the world. This is a complete waste of time and counterproductive. Don't go there!

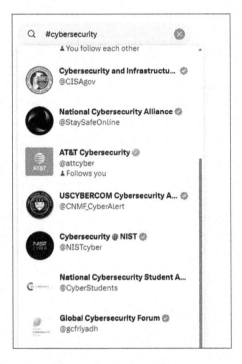

Figure 4.4 *Searching for cybersecurity topics on Twitter*

Searching for a Job

Before you start job hunting, let's take a moment to review your journey thus far. See Figure 4.5.

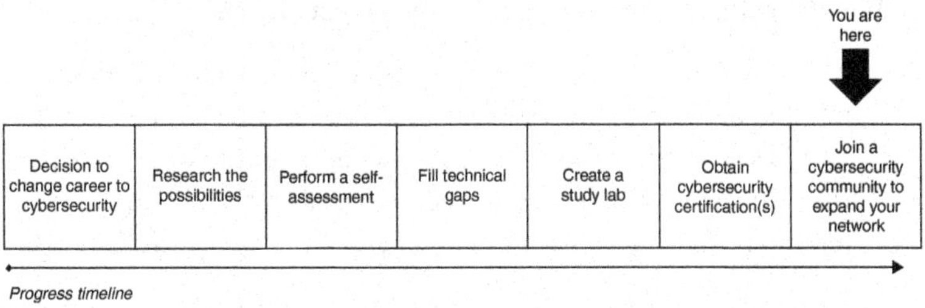

You are here

Decision to change career to cybersecurity	Research the possibilities	Perform a self-assessment	Fill technical gaps	Create a study lab	Obtain cybersecurity certification(s)	Join a cybersecurity community to expand your network

Progress timeline

Figure 4.5 *Progress timeline*

Many things were done from the point you decided to make this change until the last stage shown in Figure 4.5. If you ask me how long this process takes, my answer is, "It depends on the individual." Trying to create a "one size fits all" type of measurement is not ideal in this situation. Some people might have been unemployed when they decided to change careers, so they could accelerate some of the ramp-up, particularly in stage four (fill technical gaps) and stage five (create a study lab). Finding time to complete stages four and five will be much more challenging for someone working in a job with nothing to do with cybersecurity. But again, it all depends on how much effort you put into it. Always remember that your outcome is proportional to the effort you invest in this activity. If you handle this as a side project and only dedicate two hours a week to it, you will likely be thinking of a one-year journey just to be ready to apply for a cybersecurity job.

But let's assume you are at stage seven. You've already joined a cybersecurity community, participated in some cybersecurity projects, and gained some experience. This means it's time to update your resume before applying for a job. When updating your resume, make sure to tailor it to highlight cybersecurity-related experience. Even if you only participated for a short time, it is better to have something than nothing.

 Note

Consider using a specialized resume service such as Resume Genius to help you update your resume. See *https://resumegenius.com/*.

After updating your resume, you must make some important decisions before job hunting. Here is where you need to define how bold your next step will be and what you are really looking for. This is a critical moment because it will define your trajectory for many years to come. Here are some questions that you should ask yourself before you start job hunting:

- **Are you looking for a full-time job to complete the transition to cybersecurity or a part-time job where you can stay in your current job while gaining experience in the cybersecurity field?**

  - This is an important decision because if you currently work in a job that only occupies your first shift (for example, from 6 AM to 12 PM), why not start by adding a second-shift job in cybersecurity? This would allow you to keep your salary from your current job intact and earn a bit more in an entry-level cybersecurity job.

- **Are you able to afford a lower salary compared to your current job?**

  - This is a very common scenario when you are changing careers. It usually happens when you are already in a more senior position in your current job (which is not cybersecurity-related), but you need to start from scratch in the cybersecurity field, meaning you might have to take a pay cut in the beginning. Can you afford that? You should make this decision before you start job hunting.

- **Are you willing to move to another geo-location?**

  - Some opportunities might only be available in certain locations, and when you search without filters, you usually will get a massive amount of options because it shows open positions across the country. To facilitate your search, make sure to decide if you are willing to move or not. If you are not, it doesn't make sense to waste time looking for positions outside of the area that you are willing to live in. However, if you are willing to move for an opportunity in another country, you must find out if you need a visa sponsorship.

- **Do you want to work remotely, from the office, or a mix (also known as hybrid)?**

  - After COVID-19, the number of remote positions skyrocketed, and for many companies, it became the modus operandi for many positions. While many people love to work remotely, myself included, some people (mainly extroverts) have difficulty adjusting to working in a more isolated mode. There is no right or wrong answer here; it is really a personal choice. That's why you must ask yourself which format you prefer.

 Note

According to the 2021 American Community Survey (ACS), the number of people primarily working from home tripled between 2019 and 2021. Read more about this at *https://bit.ly/cybercareerch4link9.*

Having at least those four questions settled before you start searching for a job can help you set your own expectations and focus on your job hunting.

Now, it's time to start searching. The first question is usually, "Where do I start?" What about starting from the place where you have more connections, which at this point should be LinkedIn?

1. Open your browser and log in to LinkedIn.

2. Go to *https://www.linkedin.com/jobs/search*. There, you will find all types of jobs.

3. Type **#cybersecurity** in the search bar and click the **Search** button. Figure 4.6 shows an example of the result:

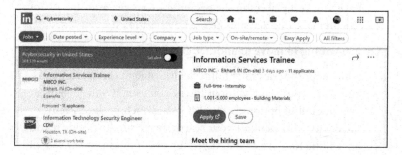

Figure 4.6 *Searching for cybersecurity jobs on LinkedIn*

4. This is a good place to start, but if you answered the questions from earlier in this chapter, you might have some restrictions, such as the job location. To change the job location, click the **All Filters** button, scroll down, and select only the places where you are willing to move.

5. Another important point to consider is whether you are willing to work remotely. Click the **On-Site/Remote** button, as shown in Figure 4-7, and select **On-Site**, **Remote**, or **Hybrid**.

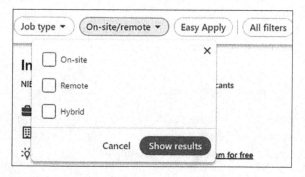

Figure 4.7 *Customizing your filter*

6. When you change the filter, the **Show Results** button also changes to show the number of jobs fitting the filter. For example, when I did this search, the **Show Results** button changed to **Show 31K+ Results**. If you look at the left side of the page shown in Figure 4-8, you will see

that the active filters are shown with green buttons. For example, in my case, it shows **Jobs** (because the main search was for **#cybersecurity**) and **Remote** (because I selected **Remote** positions only).

Figure 4.8 *Current filters*

7. One option to help you stay informed of new positions that fit these criteria is toggling the **Set Alert** slider to **On**. When this option is on, you will receive all alerts via email in a digested format that allows you to quickly see what's available, as shown in Figure 4.9.

Figure 4.9 *Email alert with jobs options*

Now is the time to review the job's requirements and expectations. In Chapter 1, we went through this exercise because you used a similar approach to identify your gaps. However, now you are more prepared because you have the knowledge and minimum experience. Although more prepared, you must be conscious of your current technical limitations and how far you can go. In other words, don't apply for jobs for which you are clearly not qualified. When recruiters see job applications from applicants who don't have the minimum requirements, they might start questioning the applicant's honesty.

Although the platform I used for this job hunt was LinkedIn, you should also consider using the following platforms:

- *Dice.com*
- *Monster.com*
- *Ziprecruiter.com*

In addition to those platforms, consider visiting the company site you want to work for. For example, if you want to work for Microsoft, visit *careers.microsoft.com* and create filters for cybersecurity-related jobs.

Summary

In this chapter, you learned the importance of building a professional cybersecurity network. You learned different approaches to expand your networking and how to engage in cybersecurity activities even if you don't work in this field full-time yet. You learned about the importance of your online presence and how to leverage it in your favor. Lastly, you learned some tips about job hunting using LinkedIn. In the next chapter, you will learn about the interview process and how to prepare.

5

Interview

Success is not final; failure is not fatal: It is the courage to continue that counts.

–Winston Churchill

I started this chapter with this famous quote from Winston Churchill because I've seen many people so afraid to fail that they don't even try. You can't think of interviewing as an all-or-nothing process because, like everything else in life, you might succeed or fail. But the experience you gained during the interview process is priceless and will be part of your journey; make sure to learn from it.

Interviewing for a cybersecurity position varies according to the position, company size, the industry, and the organization's current state. Many variables come into play, so it's important to remember that technical skills aren't everything. Over the years, I've seen many professionals hired because their soft skills were better than applicants with superior technical skills.

This chapter will teach you how to prepare for a cybersecurity interview.

Technical and soft skills

When interviewing for a cybersecurity position, you might think it's enough to have the technical skills and experience, but the ideal candidate has the complete package of experience, technical skills, and *soft skills*. Notice that I said "usually." Some positions might require a specific certification or higher education, such as a bachelor's, master's, or even a Ph.D., depending on the position you are applying for.

While these attributes can vary according to the position, one requirement is usually constant across job listings: solid soft skills. (Refer to Chapter 1 for more about soft skills.)

Interview process

Chapter 4 ended with some tips about the platforms you can use to apply for a cybersecurity position. Now let's say you applied for a job and are waiting for something to happen. Conversely, the company's recruiting team works on a pre-triage process where they review all resumes to identify which ones will go through the initial triage process.

If you are asked to set up a time for a meeting, that usually means that you passed through this pre-triage process, and now the company wants to do an initial assessment. See Figure 5.1.

 Note

The hiring process will vary according to the company and its hiring practices.

Figure 5.1 *The recruiting team selecting candidates for the interview process*

Initial triage

While the interview process might vary by company—often according to the company's size—this initial "reach out" from the recruiter is usually to chat and perform the initial triage.

Often, the hiring manager (the person who opened the position) will give recruiters a set of triage questions to determine if the candidate is ready for the interview process. These questions are usually basic—sometimes technical, and sometimes not—to evaluate whether it's worth proceeding with the formal interview process.

This initial triage interview can and usually is done online via collaborative tools such as Zoom. If the call is scheduled on a platform with video capability, make sure you are well dressed and turn your camera on unless you are explicitly told it's unnecessary.

Prepare for the interview

When you receive this initial invitation, make sure to reply with your availability and immediately start preparing for this first triage by focusing on the following aspects:

- Conduct as much research as possible about the company you are interviewing with.

- You won't look professional if the recruiter asks, "Do you know what we (the company) do?" and you have no idea.

- Go back to the position description and review everything again, including:

  - Job description

  - Responsibilities

    - Some positions will list primary and secondary responsibilities. Make sure you understand both.

  - Technical requirements (preferred and minimum)

    - Some positions will break these down into preferred and minimum requirements.

    - If you don't fulfill all the preferred technical requirements, don't panic. Make sure to take notes about which ones you lack.

    - If you have enough time to study, try to learn at least the basics (100-level) of your missing areas.

On the day of the interview, you should be relaxed but sharp. Many people have difficulty finding this balance. Don't confuse being sharp with being nervous because when you are nervous, you increase the likelihood of making mistakes. When you are sharp with a clear mind and not nervous, you are more mindful of the details and the underlying message that might occur during this interaction. This clarity allows you to think better and provide better answers. If the interview was scheduled via Zoom, Skype, or any other online conference platform, activate your camera, dress appropriately for the position you're seeking, and make sure your workspace is clean and tidy.

A study, "Initial impressions: What they are, what they are not, and how they influence structured interview outcomes," by Bryan Swider and colleagues at Scheller College of Business, Georgia Institute of Technology, concluded that interviewees who made a good initial impression during the interview received better scores for the questions they answered than those who made a poor first impression. This initial impression includes your appearance, body language, and how you articulate your ideas (communication skills). As psychology professor James Uleman, Ph.D., said, "You don't get a second chance to make a first impression."

 Note

You can read this study at *bit.ly/cybercareerch4link10*. Learn more about making a good first impression at *bit.ly/cybercareerch4link13*.

Remember that making a good first impression applies to all interview rounds. If you pass this initial triage and other interview rounds are scheduled, you should stay consistent with your posture and behavior. This is very important because after all rounds are done, the team will discuss the candidates they selected. If you behave differently each round, the interviewers will identify this unbalanced behavior, which will be a negative point for you.

1:1 WITH THE AUTHOR: THE POWER OF ENTHUSIASM

I remember when I was invited to be part of the interview panel for a position that was going to be open in Europe. This position required customer interaction, problem-solving, and a solid foundation in cybersecurity. We were willing to allow the candidate time to ramp up with the technology as long as all other attributes were on point. The recruiting team had already selected the candidates, and my job was just to interview them, write my feedback, and meet with the team to decide who was the best candidate.

It was an interesting experience because all candidates were very different in style, and most were very well prepared from a technical standpoint. But, as we went through many rounds with all these candidates, a specific one caught our attention. She was super energetic, enthusiastic about the job, and very talkative. It felt like we'd known each other for months and could've spent hours talking.

When we gathered to discuss our choices, we all shared the same perception about this candidate and thought she was the right one for this job. She hit all the core prerequisites, and although she needed some extra technology ramp-up time, her enthusiasm, passion, and energy were so contagious that we knew she was the best candidate. It was a unanimous decision!

This is a great example of a candidate who capitalizes on her strengths, showing high energy and commitment to be the best. Attitude is very important. If you have a contagious, positive attitude and are committed to learning what you don't know, you can increase your likelihood of being hired.

The important point is that she became a great security product manager who continues to deliver great results. Her enthusiasm and passion weren't just for show in the interviews. She continued to carry on and delivered great results.

Formal interview rounds

Once the initial triage is completed, the recruiter will likely send the feedback to the hiring manager, who then requests that the formal interview process start, which is usually composed of multiple interview rounds.

Each interview usually focuses on different sets of competencies that might have different sets of expectations according to the role's level, as shown in Table 5.1.

Table 5.1 Job competencies

Competency	Description	Role level	Expectation (1 to 10)*
Adaptability	The capacity to effectively adapt according to demands and circumstances while maintaining a constructive attitude.	Senior	8
Collaboration	Able to effectively work in a team environment and drive alignment across the team to achieve the company's goal.	Principal	10
Customer focus	Be empathetic about customers' needs and be a customer's advocate to ensure the issue is resolved.	Junior	5

Scale from 1 to 10, where 10 is the highest expectation, and 1 is the lowest expectation.

Technical excellence is another competency that is sometimes covered by only one interviewer. However, some companies and some cybersecurity positions might have technical questions embedded in each interview round. In this case, each interviewer will usually ask technical questions from a different angle. Table 5.2 provides some examples of multiple questions for the same position asked by different interviewers.

Table 5.2 Sample interview questions

Job position	Angle	Question
Cloud Security Architect (Senior Level)	This interviewer is looking more from the implementation angle.	Which security controls would you recommend implementing to ensure data integrity at rest in my cloud storage account?

Job position	Angle	Question
	This interviewer is looking more from the solution-designing angle.	What solution would you recommend for managing the security posture of workloads located in AWS and Azure, and what's the rationale behind choosing this solution?
	This interviewer is looking more from the integration with other tools angle.	How would you ensure all activity logs from my Azure workload are funneled to a third-party SIEM solution?

The point here is that you must be prepared to receive technical questions in all interview rounds. Understanding this possibility will help you have the right frame of mind, and if a technical question arises, you will be mentally prepared to deal with it.

Some recruiters might prefer to schedule back-to-back meetings where you finish one interview, rest for 15 minutes, and start another. When this happens, be ready to stay busy for at least four hours straight. This is particularly true when the company sponsors you for an on-site interview, which can happen in large organizations. If that's the case, make sure you stay fresh and hydrated, so you have the same enthusiasm and attitude in all interview rounds.

One important tip is that if one interview round doesn't go well, don't switch to panic mode. The worst thing you can do is jeopardize the other interview rounds because you believe you didn't do so well in the first one. The interviews are like a football game. You need to gain yards in every round. You might get stuck in some rounds, but you must go full power on to the next one. Remember that at the end, all interviewers will discuss their perceptions, meaning that one interviewer usually can't rule out a candidate if the other interviewers say positive things about the candidate. Stay focused and motivated. Don't rest when you're done with one round. Rest when your final interview for the day is finalized.

The interviewer will usually be very empathetic and try to make you comfortable so you can perform at your best. No, this is not a trick. The interviewer truly wants you to feel comfortable. The point here is to stay comfortable while being mindful of the interviewer's questions. Ask if the interviewer can repeat the question when in doubt. I've often asked one question only to have the candidate answer another question. This could be because the candidate didn't really understand what I was asking, or the candidate didn't know the answer and derailed in a different direction. Whatever the reason, if you are not sure about the question, ask the interviewer to restate it.

Figure 5.2 *Don't let your mind wander between interview rounds. Stay focused!*

 Tip

Make sure to take notes after each interview round. Reflect on what you believe you did well and what you believe can be improved. If you had to pass on a question because you didn't know the answer, make sure to research more about that question so you learn from it. If the interviewer gave you feedback during the interview, reflect on those points to see how you can improve.

Interview questions

An interviewer can take different approaches when evaluating a candidate's skills (technical and soft). Their approach is often dictated by the role for which you are applying. For example, if you are applying for an incident responder (IR) position, you need to be able to

- Stay calm under pressure
- Demonstrate excellent problem-solving skills
- Demonstrate critical thinking while investigating an incident

The question style plays a big role in determining which candidate performed better, so if you apply for an IR job, expect to be put under pressure.

Scenario-based questions about experience and skills

In this situation, the interviewer describes a scenario—design, troubleshooting, or customer temperature—and asks your opinion about it.

The common theme here is that you have a situation to resolve. Show me how you approach and solve this problem. Here are some question examples:

- You need to implement a solution that detects potential attempts to RDP brute-force a VM and automatically create firewall rules to block the source IP of the attack. What solution would you use?

- A customer opened a new incident with slow Internet browsing as the only symptom. How do you troubleshoot this?

This second scenario might have multiple interactions because it is a troubleshooting scenario. In other words, you might answer with some procedures, and the interviewer might say, "Okay, I'm the customer, I did all that, and the issue persists. What's next?" That's when you need to stay calm, think through the situation, and come up with a new set of procedures to test.

Remember that troubleshooting often eliminates hypotheses, mainly when you don't have logs to analyze. Depending on the role you are applying for, this interaction can take the entire hour of the interview. It really depends on how deep the troubleshooting goes and how deep the interviewer is willing to test your knowledge.

An in-person interviewer might ask a question that uses a drawing board approach to draw a network topology or architectural diagram to establish the scenario and then ask questions about it (see Figure 5.3).

Figure 5.3 *Drawing diagrams in an in-person interview is a common approach.*

Direct questions

In this situation, the interviewer will ask a direct question based on your experience (since they have read your resume) or your understanding of a specific topic that is a prerequisite for the job. For example:

- What does *collaboration* mean to you?

- What are the principles of Zero Trust?

- Explain what cloud security posture management (CSPM) is.

Be concise when answering direct questions. In other words, avoid being verbose to not cause fatigue. Sometimes, overexplaining can distract the interviewer and inadvertently show that you cannot explain something comprehensively.

Previous experience

In this situation, the interviewer wants you to tell a story about a past experience that matches a specific scenario. Don't create a scenario just to satisfy the request. The problem with creating a scenario that never existed is the potential follow-up question you might have to field for your made-up answer.

If the interviewer asks a follow-up question about that scenario right after your answer, you will have to create something on the fly, and if the interviewer thinks you are making things up, deeper questions will follow. If you haven't experienced that scenario, be honest and say something like, "I haven't experienced this scenario yet; can you please give me another scenario?" or you could also say: "I haven't experienced this scenario yet, but if I did, I would handle it like…." This second answer could be a good way to show your willingness to think the situation through and provide your best answer. Here are some examples:

- Tell me about a situation where you resolved a problem after a bad escalation where the customer was really upset, but you reverted the situation, and the customer was happy in the end.

- Describe your most recent experience working in a remote environment where you needed to influence others to achieve a common goal.

- Tell me about a situation where you were leading a project with an individual who was not collaborating, causing delays to the entire team. What did you do to address this situation and successfully deliver the project?

In this type of question, you might be evaluated in multiple competencies, including collaboration, leadership, level of influence, judgment, technology, and so on. Your answer might encompass many of your qualities, so make sure to be humble.

Fictitious scenario

In this situation, the interviewer will come up with a fictitious scenario where they either put you in a position of power to make decisions or pressure you to see how you behave.

Remember that this is completely fictitious, so you might have never experienced such a situation. Be thoughtful about your answer. Be creative and apply critical thinking. Here are some examples:

- Let's say the CEO of your company asked you to devise a plan to migrate all workloads to the cloud in the next 12 months. The CEO said the budget is not a problem, but you must convince key stakeholders to move their workloads to the cloud. What would you do?

- You are under pressure to finalize the project in the next 10 days, and you need leadership (LT) support to make this happen. What would you do to convince the LT?

Final decision

After all the interviews, the recruiter might initially contact you to say that the hiring manager is making a decision and will get back to you soon. Remember that this is not a rule of thumb. Each company has different hiring practices. Some might even say nothing for weeks and then come back to you with the final decision.

Although it can be frustrating, some companies might simply say you were not selected without providing any feedback. If that happens, always be respectful and express your gratitude for being part of the interview process. If no reason was given for you not being selected, you can always send a follow-up email asking for further feedback. Express that you want to learn more about the areas where you need improvement and that any feedback is appreciated.

If you were given feedback about why you weren't selected for a position, do your self-assessment to identify which areas you believe you need to improve. As mentioned earlier, you should have taken notes at the end of each round, and now is the time to look at them to determine how you can get better. You can use the flow suggested in Figure 5.4 for this continuous improvement process.

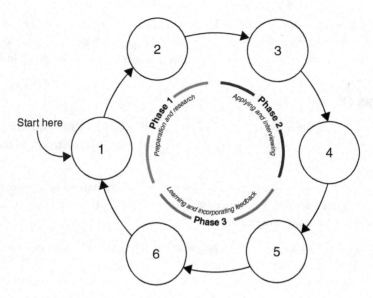

Figure 5.4 *Job hunting cycle*

Let's take a closer look at the different steps of each phase represented in Figure 5.4:

- Phase 1

    - Step 1: Deciding to look for a cybersecurity job: Understand your current skills, decide which role within cybersecurity fits your profile, perform a self-assessment to identify gaps, and establish a plan to fill those gaps.

    - Step 2: Research where you want to work, which companies you want to apply to, what type of job you want to apply for (in-person, remote, or hybrid), and understand the benefits package for those companies.

- Phase 2

    - Step 3: Apply for the jobs you identified at the end of phase 1.

    - Step 4: Start the interview process for the jobs you were selected for.

- Phase 3

    - Step 5: Learn as much as you can at each interview round, ask questions, and stay curious. Take post-interview notes to identify areas of improvement.

    - Step 6: Establish an improvement plan based on what you learned from this experience.

While many cybersecurity positions are open, the competition is tough, so you might have to repeat these six steps multiple times. Don't be discouraged by the interview results. Use each failed attempt as a learning opportunity to improve yourself.

If you did get hired, what's next? That's exactly what this book's second part will cover.

Summary

In this chapter, you learned about the interview process, technical and soft skills, and how the initial triage happens. You also learned about career competencies and the different styles of questions that might appear during an interview. In the next chapter, you will start the second phase of this book, where you will learn more about how to keep progressing in your career after you get hired.

II

On the Job

6 Your Employer Is Your Customer 99

7 Dealing with Obstacles 111

8 Growing in Your Career as a Remote Worker 127

9 What's Next in Your Career? 139

10 Owning a Cybersecurity Business 149

6

Your Employer Is Your Customer

If I had asked my customers what they wanted, they would have said a faster horse.

—Henry Ford

Now that you have started your new job in cybersecurity, you will see that there are many things to learn, which can be overwhelming. This is a very common feeling, and although it gets better over time, you will never know everything there is to know about cybersecurity. You will face many uncomfortable situations, so you change your mindset, viewing your employer as your customer instead of just where you work.

In other words, do your best to satisfy your customer and create a good relationship with them. It is about strengthening your brand regardless of the circumstances. Make your brand strong so your influence on the management chain continues increasing.

In this chapter, you will see the role of cybersecurity professionals, the importance of having top-down sponsorship to see changes, and how to have more influence on the business.

Cybersecurity Goes Beyond Technology

When cybersecurity professionals begin their careers, they commonly think cybersecurity is all about "hacking stuff." While it looks and sounds cool to advertise yourself as an ethical hacker, this will only lead you to advance in certain technical positions, and cybersecurity has more opportunities to grow than just pure technical positions. If you want to continue to grow in the cybersecurity field at your current company, you act as an enabler rather than a blocker. Your agenda needs to drive awareness rather than fear and proactive protection rather than reactive measures.

This becomes even more critical when working as a cybersecurity professional in a non-tech company like a bank or hospital where cybersecurity is not the company's core business. You need to understand that your cybersecurity decisions and policies should not negatively affect how the business operates, while you need to help secure the business to avoid disruptions caused by potential cybersecurity attacks.

As you start this new job in cybersecurity, you also need to take some time to know more about your team, understand every role, and learn how you can add value. Diversity adds value to the team, meaning your unique perspective is valuable, and you should feel empowered to share your thoughts.

1:1 WITH THE AUTHOR: DIVERSITY IN CYBERSECURITY

I could reference many studies proving the importance of diversity in cybersecurity. Instead, I will share my perspective based on having worked on teams with a wide variety of people with different backgrounds, ethnicities, nationalities, and experiences. Because to me, diversity is a very wide term that must aggregate many attributes beyond gender and race.

One of the main advantages of having a team of cybersecurity professionals with different backgrounds is that the team can come together to form their own perspective. Most of the teams I've worked with have been quite diverse, so when we brainstormed for solutions to a problem, it was always interesting to see someone else's perspective because they see things through their own lenses. Because I hadn't lived their realities, I couldn't really say, "I know what you mean." Each team member's testimonial was unique, meaning they could share things from a perspective I didn't have.

Cybersecurity teams benefit from these unique experiences to help ensure better defenses are created to mitigate potential attack scenarios. As much as you know about technology or cybersecurity, there will always be opportunities for you to learn about another's incident experience, how the incident circumstances occurred, and how to use those lessons to improve your overall security posture.

In December 2008, my team was dealing with the Conficker outbreak and had a temporary solution for U.S. customers but couldn't push the same solution to some customers in South America. Because I am from Brazil, my team asked why the workaround was not well accepted in that region, so I had to educate them about the customer mindset of that region, how they perceived the workaround, and the approach we should have been using to convince them to implement the workaround. This shows how powerful diversity can be in a global crisis where you must solve a global problem. If you only focus on your local customer, you may miss the opportunity to have a bigger impact.

Regardless of your background, you need to advocate for diversity in cybersecurity if you want to ensure the organization you work for is better prepared to deal with different threat actors.

You can learn more about Conficker in a blog post I published in January 2009 at http://bit.ly/cybercareerch4link14.

Organizational Structure

Part of knowing what everyone on your team does is understanding the organizational structure. Many people are only interested in their organizational structure when they need something. Being proactive from the beginning to better understand the entire chain of command will help you to make connections, and when you need support for a project or sponsorship for a promotion, having the right connections across the organization helps make those advancements because people will know about the work you do.

To better illustrate an organizational structure and help you navigate an organization structure where cybersecurity is an enabler for other departments, let's use the fictitious organization chart shown in Figure 6.1.

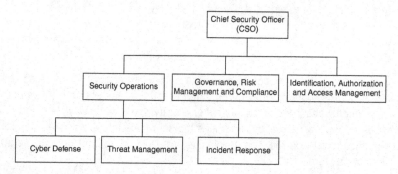

Figure 6.1 *Sample organizational chart of the information security division*

For this example, you are part of the cyberdefense team, and your job title is cybersecurity analyst junior. Your team has seven members:

- 1 cybersecurity manager
- 2 principal-level cybersecurity analysts
- 2 senior-level cybersecurity analysts
- 2 junior-level cybersecurity analysts (including you)

Your team has the following responsibilities:

- Monitoring and prioritizing security improvements for the company's assets (on-premises and cloud)
- Establishing a holistic view of the organization's attack surface and ensuring that security controls are in place to mitigate the risks
- Applying guardrails to enforce your organization's standards and policies.

Looking at this organizational structure, you can see multiple opportunities to grow within the company. Sometimes, the growth is based on lateral movement, meaning you leave one team for another without changing your compensation plan. This is considered growth because if you choose to make this transition, there is a goal behind the decision. Perhaps you want to learn different cybersecurity skills (growing your skill set) or look for long-term growth opportunities. Stay open-minded about job opportunities and don't only measure growth based on an increased salary. Always look at the broader picture to see all the indirect gains you will have with this new path you are about to choose.

Now that you understand your role and the team's responsibilities, let's see how you can navigate this organization and continue making career improvements.

Responsibilities and Expectations

One of the first things you need to do when starting a new cybersecurity job is to understand your responsibilities and expectations for your job level. The initial conversation with your manager should help bring clarity to those areas, but in doubt, you can always ask these two key questions:

- What are my responsibilities on this team?

- What are the expectations for my level?

Usually, your responsibilities will be more precise tasks you can track to see whether you deliver, such as

- Automating the vulnerability assessment process for all production servers located in the financial sector subnet

- Reviewing daily security recommendations and assigning them to workload owners

- Monitoring security posture management improvement for cloud workloads and creating a weekly report to track progress

These tasks are very precise, so when you have this level of clarity, you know exactly what you are responsible for and how to track progress. The expectations can be more subjective because expectations per role must be generic to apply to many individuals on the same level. For example, the expectations for a junior-level cybersecurity analyst might be as follows:

- Soliciting feedback and understanding their experiences across teams

- Effective communication skills

- Good operational hygiene

As you can see, these expectations are very generic and subjective because you may think you have good operational hygiene, but your manager may think you need improvement in this area. For this reason, it is important to revisit those expectations at least once a month to obtain feedback on how you are doing and what can be done better. Make sure to strive for feedback, and don't take it personally if you hear something you dislike. Your goal is not to argue with your manager when they give you disagreeable feedback. You must show a growth mindset and be willing to receive criticism that can help you grow.

 Note

Operational hygiene may mean different things in different companies. If you are a cybersecurity support professional, this may mean keeping your notes up to date in your CRM system to ensure that it reflects your last interaction with your customer.

Mapping Your Responsibilities

When you are new to cybersecurity, the initial list of tasks may be overwhelming at first. While it's normal to feel overwhelmed, you can control how you respond by understanding the skills necessary for the different parts of each task.

- If you have never done vulnerability assessment at scale and must plan the automation task for it, you must answer many questions even before you even start. Let's use the first responsibility from above as an example: Automating the vulnerability assessment process for all production servers located in the financial sector subnet. Ask the following questions:

- Is there already a vulnerability assessment process in place today in this company?

- If there is, what tool is used to perform this assessment?

- Because the request is to automate the process, how was it done today — manually or scheduled?

 Tip

Don't be shy about asking questions. You must vocalize your concerns and raise questions if you aren't clear on what needs to be done.

Once you have answers to those questions, you can start mapping your responsibilities to your skills by using an approach like the one shown in Figure 6.2. Use a drawing board as you brainstorm these responsibilities and the necessary skills to perform those tasks.

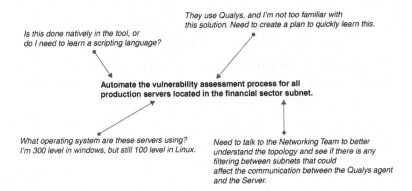

Figure 6.2 *Mapping your responsibilities with your skills and follow-up questions*

In the example shown in Figure 6.2, you have the same responsibility, but now you are looking at the keywords that will lead you to reflect on the skills necessary to perform that part of the task and assist you in reflecting on potential follow-up questions to bring even more clarity for you and your team.

Plan to Conquer

Now that you have full clarity of your responsibilities and know which skills are necessary to learn to get the work done, you need to create a realistic ramp-up plan for you and your manager. Your manager will probably give you a timeline for when they want this task done, and you will need to negotiate some extra time for you to ramp up your knowledge. For example, if this task needs to be in the next 30 days, you need to adjust your schedule to include this ramp-up phase, which could be a couple of days or one entire week, depending on your current level of knowledge about the subject.

The plan-creation exercise from Chapter 2 will come in handy now because you can use a similar structure and use Microsoft Planner to create this ramp-up plan. Here are some of the things that you need to include in this plan:

- **Ramp-up time for each technology you don't know yet:** If there are tools and/or technologies you are not familiar with, make sure to include some time to learn more about them.

- **Proof of Concept (PoC):** Once you fulfill your technical skills, you can add some time to do a PoC and validate the solution you are about to implement. This could be done in a lab to avoid affecting production. Based on the lab results, you can create a plan of action to implement in production.

- **Implementation:** Reserve some time to write down the core steps you will need to execute to implement the solution and then implement it.

- **Post-deployment notes:** Add time to document the deployed solution, the lessons you learned through this process, the potential issues you faced, and how you fixed them.

The diagram shown in Figure 6.3 shows an example of this plan.

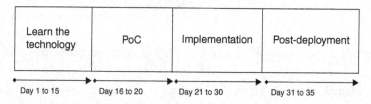

Learn the technology	PoC	Implementation	Post-deployment
Day 1 to 15	Day 16 to 20	Day 21 to 30	Day 31 to 35

Figure 6.3 *Project timeline*

While this exercise was done using just one of the three tasks given as an example earlier in this chapter, you can use the same approach for any task. The good thing is that once you create this breakdown for one task, you can use the template to plan the execution of the other tasks. This is one of the reasons that it is so important for you to organize your ideas and take notes at the end of each activity. These notes can help you learn where to improve your overall experience in the next task.

Entrepreneur Mindset

Earlier in this chapter, I briefly introduced the idea of treating your employer as your customer. Now that you are more familiar with the company that you are working for, you already understand the organizational structure, your responsibilities, and expectations, it's time to revisit the "your employer is your customer" theme.

You might be an individual contributor at your company, but if you start using an entrepreneurial mindset, you will have a bigger impact and advance in your career. Instead of thinking that your employer is demanding you to accomplish tasks A, B, and C, think of yourself as a separate company hired to do these tasks. And because you want to keep your customer happy, you want to deliver the best possible result.

Often, opportunities to do bigger and more impactful things are found in simple tasks that can be capitalized on to positively affect the business. Continue to exercise creative thinking, and when your manager asks you to do something, see how you can deliver what you've been asked to do, plus a little more. Make sure this "little more" is strategically aligned with the business and will be perceived as a positive addition to the requested task. Also, make sure to incorporate the following characteristics as part of your work ethic:

- **Ideas are not enough**: Having ideas is good, but ideas without execution don't bring tangible value to the business. To have a real impact on the business, you must turn ideas into reality and drive actions to implement your ideas. So, instead of jumping in during every meeting to say you have an idea, think about how this idea can become a reality, and then deliver a draft plan for how to turn the idea into action.

- **Be a leader**: You don't need to be in a leadership position to demonstrate your leadership skills. You can show leadership skills in how you drive projects and remove roadblocks to ensure the team is moving forward. Also, influencing leadership to get on board with your plan shows your leadership potential.

- **Learn how to collaborate and delegate**: While you will need to tackle more things on your own at the beginning of your cybersecurity career, you will learn how to delegate effectively in time. On top of that, collaboration must be part of your DNA. No one is auto-sufficient; we all must leverage other people's skills to conquer a common goal.

Incorporating these characteristics into your daily activities will improve your results and show your level of commitment to the company, which is something appreciated by managers.

When you combine these characteristics with the positive attitude of someone who is always trying to find solutions rather than problems, you have a great recipe for success. Many cybersecurity professionals focus only on bad news—and often, this is part of the job—but you need to also think about how to overcome that bad news. In order words, how can you communicate bad news with an attitude that shows your commitment to provide the best possible option to move forward in the face of adversity? That's when things take a different turn regarding how people perceive you as a professional. See Figure 6.4.

Figure 6.4 *Great attitude changes people's perception of you.*

1:1 WITH THE AUTHOR: LEVERAGE YOUR UNIQUE TALENT

I watched an interview with Steve Jobs where he said one of the greatest things he did during college was taking a calligraphy class. He was amazed by the artistry of fonts, which translated to the importance of balancing beauty with technology. He credited his concern about Apple products' visual quality and design to that experience.

We often take experiences for granted because we think something we are doing does not correlate with the "thing" we want to do in the future. Consequently, we usually don't learn about that subject because we're too busy ignoring and sometimes even completely forgetting what we have learned.

I remember a security project manager my company hired who came from a completely different background. She didn't know cybersecurity, but she knew a lot about databases and PowerBI. She started pitching ideas for dashboards that would allow us to see important data to monitor. Later, she created these dashboards. Her creativity was amazing, and while she was doing all this thinking, she was learning more and more about cybersecurity. Eventually, she became proficient in cybersecurity and created even better data analysis insights.

This is a great example of someone who took her knowledge in a different field, adapted to the needs of the cybersecurity business, and started making an impact right away. Can you imagine if, right after she joined the team, she completely ignored her previous skills and took the time to focus only on cybersecurity? It would have been a waste of talent!

Don't ignore your non-cybersecurity skills. As a matter of fact, try to see how you can leverage those skills to benefit your team, tasks, and continued growth in this field.

Summary

In this chapter, you learned how to navigate within a company's organizational structure to clarify your role and responsibilities. You learned how to prepare for new tasks and switch your mindset to work more as an entrepreneur while driving more influence and impact. In the next chapter, you will learned more about dealing with obstacles and how to overcome those situations.

7

Dealing with Obstacles

The mind adapts and converts to its own purposes the obstacle to our acting. The impediment to action advances action. What stands in the way becomes the way.

–Marcus Aurelius

In 2020, I suffered a major foot injury during a Brazilian Jiu-Jitsu tournament in Houston, Texas. That injury completely changed my life because I couldn't walk for almost three months after surgery. After the surgery, I had difficulty adjusting my schedule while facing my physical limitation to move and do simple things. During that time, I started reading more about stoicism as a philosophy and a way of living. The first book I read was *The Obstacle Is the Way: The Timeless Art of Turning Trials into Triumph* by *Ryan Holiday*. It was there that I first saw the Marcus Aurelius quote above. This book opened my mind to a different way of dealing with setbacks, hooking me on stoicism. The next book I read was *How to Think Like a Roman Emperor: The Stoic Philosophy of Marcus Aurelius* by *Donald Robertson*. Later, I had the opportunity to interview Donald in my *Overcome* podcast.

The goal of this chapter is not to fully utilize stoicism to deal with setbacks but incorporate some key elements of stoicism to help you during difficult times. Working in the cybersecurity field can be very stressful at times, impacting the quality of your work and compromising you as a professional. You need to operate under pressure with the same calm as you would without any pressure.

 Note

Interviewing Donald Robertson was fascinating. You can watch the entire *Overcome* podcast episode at https://bit.ly/cybercareerch3link16.

Obstacles in Cybersecurity

Deep Instinct's "Voice of SecOps Report 2022" found that 45 percent of respondents have considered quitting the cybersecurity industry because of stress. While many professionals think cybersecurity is stressful only if you work on a security operations (SOC) team, this report shows that C-suite jobs (like the chief information security officer) are also among those with high stress levels. This makes a lot of sense because one group (SOC) is stressed by the high attack volumes they must deal with daily, and the other group (C-suite) needs to ensure they are making the right decisions to keep the company safe. The report also reveals that cybersecurity professionals are betting on artificial intelligence (AI) to be the equalizer and help SOC analysts triage alerts and hunt threats. Eighty-two percent of the respondents said they would rather depend on AI than humans to hunt threats.

 Note

You can read more about the "Voice of SecOps Report 2022" report at https://bit.ly/cybercareerch3link17.

This report paints a good picture of cybersecurity, and you shouldn't be scared about your career change. Instead, you should be excited because the opportunity to do great things and have a bigger impact lies in the middle of chaos. But, to do that, you need to be mentally prepared. If you are not mentally prepared, you will soon be part of this statistic of cybersecurity professionals trying to leave this field because of stress (see Figure 7.1).

Figure 7.1 *Stressful situations in the Cybersecurity Field are expected*

If you look a bit deeper into some of the reasons that lead cybersecurity professionals to feel stressed at their jobs, you will see that many of the reasons are basically the nature of the business. For example, dealing with the constant evolution of threats and how to mitigate them is an ongoing process. As I've said throughout this book, you will be learning new things daily, no matter how senior you are in this field. This is the nature of the business and one reason it is challenging and rewarding.

Also, it is not only about SOC and C-level jobs. Even cybersecurity analysts can be stressed because they are frustrated with their employers for not investing enough in cybersecurity. Sometimes, analysts don't feel empowered to make decisions to improve the company's overall security posture. This is indeed a stressful situation, but again, how stressful is it on you?

One of the main lessons I learned as I studied more about stoicism is that you should not stress yourself about things beyond your control. Ancient Roman stoic philosopher Seneca said, "There is only one way to happiness, and that is to cease worrying about things which are beyond the power of our will." When you apply this principle to your professional career, you will see results in your overall quality of life. If you create an assessment report categorizing all risks and mitigations, but your manager has decided to postpone the mitigations because there is no budget coming this quarter to invest in this area, you have no reason to stress yourself. You did your job, documented your findings, wrote a great report, and presented it to the leadership. They acknowledged the problem and decided to assume the risk. Done. Your part is completed — time to move on to the next thing, even if the next thing is trying to bring awareness about the same problem!

I understand the feelings of "mission not accomplished," frustration, and powerlessness. Those are reasonable feelings, but it's not about your feelings but how you will deal with those feelings and move on. You can hold those feelings inside of you and move on, but when the same thing happens again, you will bring up all those old feelings on top of the current frustration, and then you will have the final feeling of "I'm done!"

Obstacles will always show up on your way, often stopping you from moving forward. How you deal with that defeat is really what will define you. You may stumble at first, but you get back up, learn from that defeat, and try to do better next time. If the company didn't approve your budget this time, what can you do differently next time to get more attention? Maybe you need to create a virtual team (v-team) and get more opinions to show your leadership and influence skills. You must be creative, use critical thinking instead of emotional thinking, and learn how to influence your leadership despite the setbacks that you may have had on the first attempt.

Also, make sure to practice gratitude for the things you already have and already accomplished. Gratitude changes our perspective of things and helps us stay grounded in what matters. Practice that daily, and your perception of things will change; as a result, your approach to dealing with obstacles will also change.

1:1 WITH THE AUTHOR: DON'T TAKE THINGS PERSONALLY

One of my former managers and this book's technical reviewer always challenged us to stretch ourselves by creating goals we might never achieve, but we would learn something along the way. We had many discussions about these goals because it was always hard for me to digest the idea of creating a goal that I couldn't achieve. Since 2013, I've been using SMART Goals (as discussed in Chapter 2).

In one of those heated discussions, he said: "Don't worry. I don't take things personally. You can vent as much as you want." That was very good to hear because I really wanted to feel safe to disagree and make my point. Because of that, I also told the people who worked for me that I didn't take things personally and that there was always a safe space to talk, criticize, and come up with a solution. Even if that solution wasn't my preferred option, I was all in if they convinced me this was the best solution for the business.

Adopting this mindset alleviates a lot of pressure and helps you avoid the anxiety that comes with hearing someone disagree with you. Heated discussions are expected, and as long as they are respectful and professional, then there is nothing wrong.

Also, remember that when working in a diverse group, different people with different backgrounds may behave differently based on their culture. Some people from some cultures tend to be very direct, which can be misconstrued as rudeness. Rather than viewing their directness as rude, I learned to view it as them being straightforward. I learned it was better to have things out in the open instead of dealing with hidden agendas.

On the other hand, if you take everything personally, a little change in your environment might make you feel like someone is trying to stab you in the back. This will often lead others to perceive you as someone who overreacts and is not mature enough to deal with setbacks. Remember that you can't control every situation, but you can control how you react to that situation, and this is critical for your professional growth. A mindset where you always take things personally will not help you in the long run, and it will decelerate your growth in this field and create even more obstacles for you to deal with.

Unconscious Bias and Cybersecurity

Unconscious bias—also known as implicit bias—are assumptions, social stereotypes, beliefs, or attitudes that are difficult to control because they exist beyond our conscious thoughts but are dangerous because they can affect how we act.

Unconscious bias in cybersecurity can affect your capacity to investigate incidents, how you read and interpret the data, and how you make decisions that will have a broader impact. A common unconscious bias in cybersecurity is always blaming the user for everything. While many professionals say this is a joke, your subconscious will maintain that correlation, and at some point, when you are trying to justify why something went wrong, you may tend to say it is the user's fault. See Figure 7.2.

Figure 7.2 *Always stay alert about your own bias when making decisions*

But there are other types of bias. Let's say you are a cybersecurity analyst who needs to prepare a report justifying the investment in mitigations found based on your vulnerability assessment report. At that point, your mindset may be: *I need to convince the leadership that we are in a bad situation, and they need to invest more.* This means you are narrowing your scope to find only bad things and hunting for information confirming your assumption. In other words, you are using a confirmation bias. This type of bias can affect your critical thinking because you are not considering other elements. Instead, you are validating your assumption and not thinking broadly.

Jumping to conclusions because you believe the current behavior is the same as you've experienced previously might not be beneficial because it can blind you from truly investigating and looking for more evidence before coming up with a conclusion. Experience is important—and you should consider your own experience—but don't stop there. Continue to dig and keep an open mind for other possibilities.

If you are in the threat intelligence or incident response fields, you need to be even more alert about unconscious bias. In the book *Physiology of Intelligence Analysis*, published by the Central Intelligence Agency (CIA), Center for the Study of Intelligence, the author, Richards J. Heuer Jr., suggests six steps to help intelligence analysts to improve their analytical process and reduce cognitive bias. The steps are:

- **Define the problem:** Be precise in the problem definition, and ask as many questions as possible to clarify what problem you are dealing with.

- **Generate hypothesis**: Even before collecting information, you can brainstorm with your team all the potential hypotheses for this problem.

- **Collect information**: Collect information that can be used for this investigation and ensure data is coming from different sources. The data should be used to validate the hypotheses that were brought to the table.

- **Evaluate hypothesis**: This is a tricky moment of the investigation because your unconscious bias may lead you to look for evidence confirming your own hypothesis. Don't fall into this trap. Look for evidence that can also be applied to another hypothesis, and stay open to critical thinking.

- **Select the most likely hypothesis**: You can start by eliminating a hypothesis that doesn't have sustainable evidence and keep narrowing it until you get to the most likely hypothesis.

- **Ongoing monitoring of new information**: Continue monitoring the situation because new information may arise.

 Note

You can download the *Physiology of Intelligence Analysis* ebook from https://bit.ly/cybercareerch3link18. For some good examples of cognitive bias, see https://bit.ly/cybercareerch3link19.

While these steps were proposed for intelligence analysts, they are foundational principles and can be applied in cybersecurity jobs requiring investigation and interpretation of data to come up with conclusions.

Cyberthreat intelligence analysts must deal with massive amounts of information to start understanding adversaries' behavior. In the case of post-mortem analysis, this basically means reverse-engineering the actions already done to understand the adversaries' motives and impact.

Adjusting Your Cybersecurity Skills

Another obstacle that may appear in your way is the need to learn new skills that you didn't consider in your initial assessment, but now that you are in this new job, you must adjust to fulfill this new demand. This is a common situation in the cybersecurity field because of the constant in technologies to deal with new threats and continuous improvement of security controls.

If this happens, you must show you are ready to embrace chances and learn something new. In the last chapter, we talked about the importance of your attitude, and this is exactly the moment you need to be supportive to ensure your manager and team can count on you to learn this new skill.

Let's use a cybersecurity analyst working on the blue team (defense) as an example. When this analyst was hired, the job requirements included the following activities:

- Prioritize and identify security risks, threats, and vulnerabilities

- Lead various teams to operationalize remediation efforts

- Develop and implement security monitoring roadmaps for SaaS and other cloud-hosted solutions

After six months on the job, a restructure (also known as a reorganization or reorg) merged this team with the incident response and threat intelligence teams. Now, the following requirements have been added:

- Actively monitor and research cyberthreats

- Lead monthly reporting to security management on incident metrics

- Review technical analysis of security events

- Ensure and directly oversee the collection and preservation of data associated with cybersecurity incident response activities following industry best practices

Notice that the job scope aggregates more things, which most likely will affect the daily activities and work hours. If you don't know how to deal with this, it will add a lot of stress to your life. Not only will you need to learn new skills, but you also will be responsible for more things. At this point, avoid worrying about earning more money for more work. That's not how things work in companies, and most likely, you will not be seen as a professional for saying that right up front.

You need to create a plan to see how you can impact this new scope, deliver the results, and have sync-up conversations with your manager to show those positive results. As you continue to show positive results, you can start slowly introducing the business case for your promotion because you have shown flexibility to adjust yourself to new needs and excellence in delivering by ensuring that you are constantly delivering great results.

You turn a situation that could be very stressful into a business case to promote you. How's that for winning? Of course, this isn't easy—and I'm not saying you won't have headaches—but if you learn how to capitalize on each obstacle, you will increase your likelihood of success while better managing the stress and your career longevity.

What Got You Here Won't Get You There

If you receive a promotion, don't think you can continue doing the same things to get the next promotion. This approach doesn't work in a corporate environment, especially when moving up levels within the same role. The things you achieved previously become your new baseline, so you need to achieve more to continue moving up. What was a win last year is now a normal expectation.

That's why you need to ensure you and your manager understand your priorities for the next fiscal year, the areas you should focus on, and the areas you need improvement. If possible, take on assignments that allow you to have a bigger impact on the company. The worst mistake you can make is to go rogue and start doing things that you believe are great for the business, especially if those things are not aligned with your team's charter or your manager is unaware of them.

There are so many opportunities in the cybersecurity field that it is very common for you to feel empowered to just start doing things that, in your mind, are important but are not aligned with your team's goals.

Work-Life Balance in Cybersecurity

By this point of the chapter, you might wonder if it's even possible to have a work-life balance (WLB) in cybersecurity. Absolutely! But a lot of this work-life balance ("work-life harmony," as Jeff Bezos refers to it) will depend on how you handle your tasks, your agenda, your overall time management, and how you create healthy habits for yourself.

 Note

You can read more about the rationale behind Jeff Bezos's work-life harmony theory here: https://bit.ly/cybercareerch3link23.

A lot of professionals are very passive regarding work-life balance. They expect their manager or even their companies to tell them what to do. WLB starts with you taking control of your own life and creating boundaries to avoid work overflowing into your personal life.

1:1 WITH THE AUTHOR: THE DANGEROUS SIDE EFFECTS OF TUNNEL VISION

When I started working full-time in cybersecurity in 2007, I was part of a team supporting incident response for our customers. The team had many specialization areas, and my specialization was in edge security (firewall). I was fascinated by the work, the product, the team, and the information I learned daily.

Not only was the excitement high, but I was also very determined to continue to grow in my career. So, I put in a lot of extra hours studying, taking relevant certifications, and spending extra hours at work to do more. My shift started around 1 PM and was supposed to end around 9 PM. However, our U.S. group was the escalation point for Europe and Asia, so after 5 PM our time, we started receiving many escalations. If we didn't resolve them, we had to stay working until India could take over, which usually was around 9 PM. In theory, things should work smoothly, but in practice, not so much, as I often had to stay on calls until midnight before handing it over to India.

This tunnel vision, where I was 100 percent focused only on work, resulted in two promotions in three years and the opportunity to sign my first contract with Microsoft Press to write my first book in English—a book about Microsoft Forefront Threat Management Gateway (TMG). But I paid a high price for this tunnel vision.

Due to my lifestyle, I gained around 100 pounds and started to have health issues as I became morbidly obese. My lab results were terrible, I felt terrible, and I didn't have time to spend with my family at home. In 2011, I realized that I needed to change because, as my doctor at that time said, if I didn't change, I wouldn't live for too long.

I started a weight loss program and exercising more in 2011, about the time I left for a remote position with another team. I was working from home, with more control over my agenda, food, and breaks. Life changed, and I wrote a book titled *Ready, Set, Achieve!: A Guide to Taking Charge of Your Life, Creating Balance, and Achieving Your Goals*.

However, the main lesson learned in this journey was the company didn't change the WLB policy, and my manager didn't change his WLB approach. I was the one who needed to change and make sure I created a better balance. That's why it is so important to be mindful of this and avoid this tunnel vision unless you are willing to deal with the consequences that come with this approach, and most importantly, don't have any regrets.

Note

You can read more about my book, *Ready, Set, Achieve!: A Guide to Taking Charge of Your Life, Creating Balance, and Achieving Your Goals*, at https://bit.ly/cybercareerch3link20.

It is very easy to get distracted by filling up your day with work-related tasks, and then on top of that, still need to fit in your plans to learn new technologies to continue improving yourself. When you combine these aspects (constant distraction and an agenda full of things to do) with the fact that many cybersecurity professionals have computer-related habits (like playing games), you will easily find yourself in front of the computer for 20 hours a day. This will absolutely cause burnout, and the worst part is that you don't see it coming because, in your mind, this is life as usual, but then something triggers a wake-up call. And this something is usually related to your physical or mental health.

A 2022 survey of more than 1,000 cybersecurity professionals across the United States and Europe revealed that 50.8 percent of these professionals had been prescribed medications for their mental health. This is very alarming, and while the stress of the job will contribute to this result, how you handle your WLB has a big impact on your mental health.

 Note

You can read more about this survey at https://bit.ly/cybercareerch3link21.

Make no mistakes about it: Believing you need to be plugged in 100 percent of the time, getting all the cybersecurity news, studying, building your brand, and trying to grow high-impact projects is something all cybersecurity professionals suffer if they fail to handle their lives properly. I remember recording an episode of my *Overcome* podcast with David Kennedy, founder of TrustedSec and a highly achieved cybersecurity professional. He went through this burnout process, leading to weight gain, feeling miserable, and a substantial decrease in productivity. He admitted that he did all that to grow his career. However, he now says he would do it all differently—this time, without compromising his health. He also revealed that his experiences made him a big advocate for cybersecurity professionals living better lifestyles. His experiences also led him to create the *We Hack Health* podcast(follow @wehackhealth on Twitter for more information).

 Note

You can watch the entire *Overcome* podcast, where I interviewed Trusted-Sec founder David Kennedy, at https://bit.ly/cybercareerch3link22.

Growing at a Healthy Pace

It is important to understand that some moments of your professional career will demand more from you. You might be leading a strategic project that demands more work hours, or you might be in the final sprint to make a deadline. You should still be able to make those sprints without affecting your WLB in the long term because you have a baseline to control your agenda better. Deviations in your agenda will occur sometimes, but as long as you have this solid baseline of how you should operate each day, it helps to handle events that occur and are outside of your normal day.

As you have learned in this chapter, the cybersecurity field can push your limits, and this thin line between being stressed all the time and pushing yourself to grow is also tricky to manage. When is enough *enough*? Many people struggle to determine that, but it goes back to the core principle I mentioned before: you need a baseline.

There is a difference between living on the edge every day and feeling that you never have enough time. You can be mentally prepared for deviations if you have established a baseline for your daily, weekly, and monthly routines.

So, you first need to establish a healthy routine to prioritize your well-being, which includes exercise and eating healthy. Make sure that you take at least one hour each day to exercise. This recommendation is based on my experience of losing 100 pounds and gaining more brain clarity and productivity improvement, and it's supported by plenty of studies. One study shows 72 percent of the participants reported improvement in managing their time and completing their tasks at work on days that they exercised. Don't ignore this data if you want to be the best version of yourself at work.

 Note

Read more about this study at https://bit.ly/cybercareerch3link24.

Besides exercise, you must also have a well-balanced diet, with healthy food that will positively impact your brain and how you feel. Remember that food is your fuel. If you put bad fuel in your body, you will perform badly. It is that simple. I gained control of my food intake after tracking what I ate using the MyFitnessPal app, which helped me become more aware of how many non-necessary calories I consumed.

 Note

You can read more about how I use the MyFitnessPal app at https://bit.ly/cybercareerch3link25.

So, now that you have gotten your exercise and food under control, what else do you need? Enough rest. You must get a good night of sleep. The days of over-glorifying workaholics are over, and while you may need to miss some nights of sleep because of work, it should not be your norm; it should be a rare exception. We know that sleep deprivation can cause mood disorders, and nothing can be worse than being in a meeting where people expect you to come up with impor-tant ideas and solutions, but you are in such a bad mood that everything you say is negative.

With these three elements, you have a solid foundation to get started, as shown in Figure 7.3.

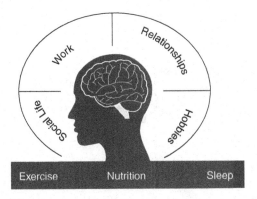

Figure 7.3 *Building a solid foundation to help in other areas of your life.*

When I wrote this chapter in 2023, the tech industry was going through a major readjustment, with the big corporations laying off thousands of people. I remember browsing through LinkedIn and watching the painful testimony of many people who lost their jobs. I saw many heartfelt "my work was my everything" testimoni-als. While I don't criticize those who regard their careers as everything in their lives, I will always warn people that their lives need to be about more than just work. The diagram shown in Figure 7.3 is a basic representation of that. Most people who don't have a good WLB suffer more when their whole world (work) collapses. This is a complex subject, and many people need to seek help from a professional counselor to deal with it. Make sure to revisit your company's human resources benefits to see if they have mental health–related support and how you can get professional help.

On the other hand, many testimonials portrayed things very differently, showing appreciation for what they learned over the years and acknowledging that life is more than work, and they feel thankful for the support from family and friends. When you have a good balance between all areas of your life, you don't feel empty if one of those areas collapses because your life is about more than just work.

Time Management

Many books go far deeper into this topic than I can go in this chapter. The goal here is to share some best practices that have worked for many of my mentees.

If you already have the good foundation that I mentioned in the previous section (exercise, nutrition, and sleep), you should always feel mentally fresh and have your overall stamina on point to get things done, which are imperative attributes when thinking about time management. The next step is to organize your weekly agenda by establishing what you want to accomplish during the current week. Another option is to block 1 hour of your calendar on Monday morning to do this planning. I prefer to do this at the end of the day on Friday. Let's use the example shown in Figure 7.4.

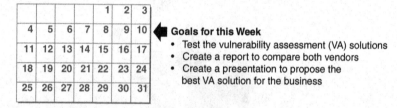

Figure 7.4 *Establishing weekly goals*

While these are this week's three main goals, you must usually address ongoing tasks while managing your primary goals. And that's where the challenge starts. It's important to establish your priorities with your manager. Nothing is really a priority if everything is priority zero because nothing will get done with quality. Once you have the list of things you need to prioritize, you must create a daily list of tasks you want to accomplish. Some tasks will directly contribute to the current week's goals; others are related to other activities you already have on your backlog.

Since we are talking about your agenda, it is very important to integrate these tasks with your schedule to block off time to perform tasks and avoid other meeting requests while you are busy executing the tasks you need to finish. If you use Microsoft Outlook, you can use the *Task* function to create your tasks, as shown in Figure 7.5.

An Outlook task allows you to establish the start and due date, the status (if you started, in progress, and so on), and the completion percentage. You can even add reminders. You should review these tasks at the end of each day to track your progress and update them accordingly.

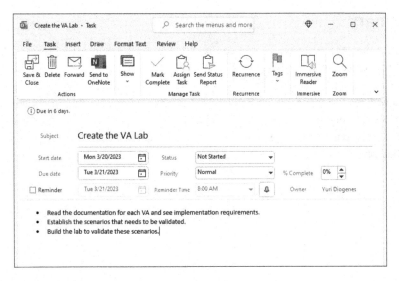

Figure 7.5 *Outlook Tasks*

The advantage of setting daily tasks is that it allows you to react faster if you see that things are not progressing. For example, if you don't see progress in one of your tasks by Wednesday, you have time to reassess to see if you need to postpone or if you need to add more hours of work before the due date to get it done.

In summary, the three main recommendations are:

- Create weekly goals.

- Prioritize your workload to understand what needs to be delivered on that week.

- Create a list of daily tasks that will help achieve the week's goals while accommodating your current backlog.

While these recommendations will help you to manage your workload better, you need to be realistic about your workload, and if you feel you don't have the bandwidth to do what you were asked to do, make sure to escalate the issue to your manager. During this conversation, make sure to share the current issues and bring suggestions for resolving them. If you don't have suggestions, say so, and ask for help. A big part of staying in a healthy mental state is acknowledging your vulnerabilities and seeking help if things are not going well. Most people I've known over the years who had mental health breakdowns were in that state because they didn't share their struggles because they were afraid of being perceived as weak. Don't be afraid to show your vulnerabilities and be open to your manager about your current roadblocks.

Summary

In this chapter, you learned about common obstacles that may arise in your cyber-security career, including unconscious bias, potential adjustments that you need to make in your cybersecurity skills to handle new demands, and adjustments that you will need to make in your deliverables as you continue to climb up in your job. You also learned the importance of keeping a good work-life balance and growing at a healthy pace. In the next chapter, you will learn more about career growth in cybersecurity as a remote worker.

8

Growing in Your Career as a Remote Worker

Perfection is not attainable. But if we chase perfection, we can catch excellence.

–Vince Lombardi

For years, the term "remote worker" had a negative connotation, but if you stay humble and understand that there's always room for improvement, you can turn your remote worker status into a positive for both you and your employer. And if you believe you're no longer learning as a remote worker, then it's time to make some changes.

Remote working became a reality after COVID-19 when the global market changed to accept remote workers and encourage people to work remotely. COVID-19 drove many companies to accelerate their digital transformation by migrating their resources to the cloud and enabling remote access to all employees. While this introduced many challenges—mainly data security—it also opened the door for many people to work for organizations anywhere in the world, regardless of where they lived.

Once established as a remote worker, how do you keep growing in your career? Many people don't realize that working remotely requires a different approach than working in the office.

The Growth of Remote Workers

Remote work grew steadily in the years leading up to 2020, but when the COVID-19 pandemic hit, working remotely reached a whole new level as companies had to adjust their workforce to allow all employees to work outside the office. While this mandatory push helped accelerate the digital transformation for many companies, it also created challenges, particularly information security. Many companies weren't ready to perform this massive shift and didn't have the necessary security controls in place, increasing cyberattacks targeting remote employees.

But with challenges also come opportunities, and even companies that were traditionally unwilling to hire remote workers for certain positions began reconsidering their strategies and opening remote positions at all levels (including director- and VP-level positions). See Figure 8.1.

According to Global Workplace Analytics, 82 percent of U.S. employees wanted to continue working from home at least once a week after the pandemic, and according to the State of Remote Work 2020, Owl Labs, 46 percent of employees would look for another job if their company doesn't allow them to work remotely. This shows that employees are happier with the flexibility of working from home and that many people are willing to look for a job that gives this flexibility rather than going back to the office 100 percent of their time.

Figure 8.1 *Remote work became a standard mode during the pandemic*

 Note

> You can read more about the Global Workplace Analytics study at https://bit.ly/cybercareerch3link27.

While this was the normal trend in 2020–2022, as things started to normalize again in 2023, companies reviewed their remote work policies and requested employees to work from the office part of the week. Mark Zuckerberg (CEO of Meta) said that according to internal analysis at Meta, the employee performance data suggested engineers who work in the office "get more done."

 Note

> You can read more about Meta's internal analysis at https://bit.ly/cybercareerch3link26.

Hybrid Work

Once companies began reviewing their remote work policy after the worst of the pandemic was over, many large corporations required employees to work in the office at least three times a week, as happened with Amazon in early 2023 when they mandated the return to the office.

 Note

You can read more about Amazon's hybrid work environment at https://bit.ly/cybercareerch3link28.

If your company starts a hybrid work program, you should show you are ready to embrace change and adapt to these new requirements. In the previous chapter, we talked about the importance of your attitude, so you need to be supportive to ensure your manager and team can count on you to adjust to this new demand. Hybrid work has advantages and disadvantages. The main advantage is the opportunity to network face-to-face again with your peers, helping build a better team. The main disadvantage is that employees must live close to the office, meaning it would not be feasible for you to work in Dallas while living in Los Angeles, eliminating a lot of the flexibility provided by full-time remote work.

The market is still unsettled on remote versus hybrid work. While many analysts say remote work is here to stay, the push to a hybrid mode is taking precedence in large corporations, requiring workers to live near the office to be physically in the office for part of the week. In 2023, we saw a massive number of layoffs in the tech industry, which also contributed to many companies revisiting their remote work policies and issuing return-to-office (RTO) mandates.

As you navigate your cybersecurity career, make sure to consider both your current company's remote work policy and that company's current trends that could affect your growth. However, regardless of whether you work fully remote or hybrid, you must understand how you can make an impact and grow in your career when you don't have this in-person experience available 100 percent of the time.

 Note

Read more about the 2023 Tech Industry Layoffs at https://bit.ly/cybercareerch3link29.

Making an Impact as a Remote Worker

When an entire team works remotely, there is a natural feeling of unsafety because everyone is remote. There are no in-person side conversations (sometimes called water cooler conversations) with people in the same building. Remote workers often feel they are missing something because part of the team works together in the same building. Naturally, remote workers worry that the in-house employees talk more often, go out to lunch together, and have more conversations than they have with remote workers.

While remote work can be challenging, you can still make an impact, but you will need to be more active. Remote workers rely on online communication to express their ideas, communicate, and influence others, meaning the following communication is critical for remote workers to dominate:

- **Email**: While many other communication methods exist, email is still the primary means. Every time you answer an email, think about the target audience and what you are trying to convey. Words are powerful, so make sure you review the email to ensure there is no doubt about the point you are trying to make. Ideally, you should anticipate follow-up questions by adding all necessary facts and data. After writing the email and before clicking Send, review it and ask yourself if you would have more questions if you had received this email.

- **Online meetings**: During the pandemic, the word we heard most about online meetings was "Zoom," as in, "I have a Zoom meeting." Camera use during meetings became commonplace and almost expected. Having your camera on during meetings is critical if you are a full-time remote worker. It makes you stay focused and avoid multitasking. Your level of engagement increases, and people feel more connected by looking at you and seeing your expressions and how you react to their comments. Keep your camera on, stay engaged, and avoid multitasking while in meetings.

- **Online chat**: Regardless of the tool your company uses for chat (Microsoft Teams, Slack, and so on), chat is the standard of communication between peers when it comes to quick information sharing, asking questions, or checking in with one another. As a full-time remote worker, this type of tool is your main ally. Your level of chat engagement shows how connected you are with your team and how responsive you are about critical topics.

In cybersecurity, it is common for professionals of all disciplines to use those tools to communicate, share findings, document reports, and follow up on top-of-mind items during meetings. Because there is an expectation that you can be effective as a remote worker using those tools, it is up to you to ensure you are vocalizing your thoughts effectively and that both your team and all stakeholders know about you. You need to expand your reach to ensure you are seen as a good team player—with your and other teams. Once established, you can expand your reach to areas outside your organization.

Once you've established your reach, you also need to increase your level of influence. This can start with how you communicate your ideas and empower others to achieve more. Don't just think about yourself when you must convince others that your plan is the right one to follow. Put your ego aside and include others in the winning package. Show how this plan will also benefit the other person you are trying to influence. Avoid going back and forth via email to discuss a topic. Make sure to choose the right method of communication for optimal influence. Written methods (email or chat) are often not the best choices. Instead, set up a quick 30-minute video meeting to have visual contact with the person you are trying to influence.

Influencing Others

In the age of big data and a colossal amount of information, it can be overwhelming for people to understand the real goal behind long email threads. One way to have a bigger impact is to bring clarity to a conversation. Sometimes, you will have to step up and be the one who summarizes the long thread and clarifies the real ask, the expectations, and the next steps.

As a remote worker, you can't shy away from discussions. You need to stay engaged and see how your communication will help everyone to move forward. Your engagement level will not always come from a technical standpoint. Your level of impact requires other skills as you continue to grow in your career. Figure 8.2 shows an example of how this happens over time:

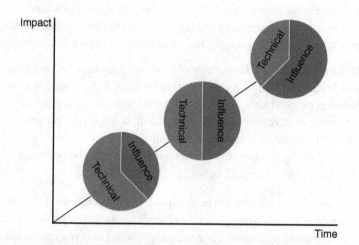

Figure 8.2 *Your level of influence becomes more important over time*

At the beginning of your career, your technical abilities were the primary skills you needed to drive a bigger impact, but as you grow, your nontechnical skills must grow with you. Eventually, your technical skills won't be as important as they were in the beginning. The influence part of the pie chart shown in Figure 8.2 contains a different set of skills that you will gain over time:

- **Actively listen to what people are saying:** There is a big difference between listening and active listening. When actively listening, you are not thinking about how to reply to every sentence; you are engaged and digesting what the person is saying. When you actively listen, people believe you care, and when people believe that you care, they tend to trust you, and trust is the first step to creating influence.

- **Be empathetic:** You must relate to another person's struggle and feelings. Showing empathy in a conversation can also increase trust, a stepping stone for influence.

- **Use your problem-solving skills:** While this is probably a skill you already have from the technical perspective, you also need to apply it to resolve conflicts and help create common ground for the team. You leverage negotiation and persuasion skills for navigation and problem-solving.

- **Motivate others:** While you can't be motivated 100 percent of the time, you can help others to overcome struggles by motivating them to keep moving forward despite the obstacles. As American memoirist, poet, and civil rights activist Maya Angelou said, "People will forget what you said, people will forget what you did, but people will never forget how you made them feel."

Another important tip for creating an empowering environment is to share your thoughts about your coworkers. This could be via a formal feedback mechanism (many companies have a formal feedback peer review tool) or just an email of appreciation. Little doses of motivation help inspire people to do more and strengthen your relationship with them. When giving kudos to others, make sure you tailor your message so it speaks to the individual. Avoid generic kudos for the sake of giving them. Be specific by sharing exactly what the individual did to deserve recognition. Lastly, make sure to emphasize how their efforts drove a positive outcome.

Actively Look for Feedback

Setting up ongoing meetings with people outside of your circle is essential as a remote worker. By scheduling monthly or even quarterly meetings with someone outside your organization with more experience helps you gain insights, exchange thoughts, and obtain feedback about your work. Make sure to choose strategic people within or outside your organization who can help you get things done because they are higher up in the organization chart, such as principal-level people, managers, or company influencers. See Figure 8.3.

Figure 8.3 *Feedback is a great tool for continuous improvement*

You should always look for areas of improvement in your work. Sometimes, you can't see these areas because you may think you are doing everything correctly. When working remotely, you don't have water cooler conversations with your peers that sometimes trigger conversations about behavior and situational awareness. As a remote worker, you must actively seek out those conversations and understand how your actions are perceived.

Sometimes, you have the best of intentions, but others do not perceive your approach well, and you may not even realize it until you have an uncomfortable conversation where you are criticized for something you didn't realize was wrong. Remote workers must be mindful of those situations, mainly during cross-team collaboration, because other team members may not know you. Be mindful of those circumstances because although you may be comfortable working remotely, someone else may struggle to work with you because they have never worked with remote employees. Again, be empathetic and a facilitator to bridge both worlds.

Staying Active

Creativity is very important for remote workers. You must be thoughtful about what is happening around you and how you can capitalize on that for the benefit of your organization. While you and your team are working toward a common goal, you can always create initiatives that will drive results faster.

Many people struggle as remote workers because they feel disconnected from the environment and don't know what to do next. Nowadays, companies seek self-motivated and self-driven individuals who can be productive with few instructions. In other words, don't expect your manager to tell you what you should do each hour of your day. Most likely, you will have certain tasks to accomplish, and it is up to you how you will get them done within your workday. Remote workers must have the discipline to stay active even if their backlog is not keeping them too busy. It is very easy to slack off when nobody is monitoring you.

Make sure to use your time wisely, and if you have big gaps during the day where you don't have much work to do, go learn something, study, think about what can be done next, and be creative. There are always opportunities to do something if you spend a little time thinking about new projects and areas you can impact. Always stay alert for crisis and turmoil scenarios. What opportunities are available because of the post-COVID shift in how people work? As mentioned many times in this book, your attitude and approach to dealing with problems will dictate much about how you continue growing in your career.

1:1 WITH THE AUTHOR: IDENTIFYING OPPORTUNITIES DURING STRESSFUL TIMES

At the beginning of COVID in early 2020, many companies started investing more in online videocasts, webinars, and podcasts. When in-person events were canceled, most conferences migrated online, leading to the rapid growth of online events.

I was personally interviewed about Azure Security Center on an online talk show. After that interview, I wondered if we should have a show dedicated to Azure Security Center, leading to the creation of my own home studio. I purchased a good camera and microphone, installed OBS Studio on my computer, and started playing around.

In July 2020, I released the first episode of *Azure Security Center in the Field*, where I interviewed product managers from the Azure Security Center team in Israel. The show became a success, with many guests lined up for future episodes, driving awareness about the product. Azure Security Center product managers began showcasing their new features on my podcast.

I released 33 episodes under the name *Azure Security Center in the Field*, and in 2021, when the product was rebranded Defender for Cloud, I rebranded the show as *Defender for Cloud in the Field*. As of April 2023, I have 29 episodes published and counting. The show is still going strong, with guests lined up for at least an entire month.

Creating this show from scratch and producing, editing, and finding advertising funds were never part of my charter, but I embraced these activities to help spread the word about Defender for Cloud. The positive collateral effect of this was a boost in my personal brand and an improvement in my personal networking. If you have a clear goal to accomplish, there will always be positive side effects that will help you personally. Always base your decisions on improving the business and positively impacting the organization.

Don't look for opportunities that benefit only you. The consequence of a good job where you accomplish your goal will be reflected in your personal growth and your personal brand improvement, so there is no need to think about how an opportunity will directly help you. Sometimes, the gain is indirect, or the benefits will be harvested down the road. In difficult times, there are always opportunities to do great things.

Looking ahead of the curve and understanding the potential situations that may arise if certain decisions are made is also a great way to stay engaged. Make sure to vocalize your thoughts when you see the possibility that going in one direction may have undesirable results. At the same time, you should always try to find a solution, not just emphasize the problem. It is not enough to say that we will fail if we go in this direction. That's good, but what direction should we go and why? By pointing out the problem and articulating the best solution, you add more value to the conversation and build more trust among your peers and managers.

Transparency

Remote workers won't have the opportunity to stop by their manager's office when they want to ask questions or provide a quick update; this is where online chat is beneficial. As a remote worker, you must be very transparent about your work and availability. There are some misconceptions that remote workers can be anywhere, and nobody cares what they're doing as long as the work gets done. This is not true, and you should not assume as much without clarifying this with your manager.

Imagine an employee spending half their day at the beach and then returning home to do some work. Although this seems to be a completely absurd example, a friend who owns a company caught his employee doing this very thing. The employee claimed to be completing their work during the remainder of the day. Even if the work was getting done, the employee had never talked about work-hour management with their manager. When you are working remotely, other people may have to reach you, and if they don't know your working hours and availability, you become known as someone hard to reach, possibly stunting your professional growth.

Transparency is the key to a good work relationship, and as a remote employee, you must take extra care of this because people don't see you physically, which means your online presence and responsiveness dictates how people perceive you. Perception is very important when it comes to your online presence and how your peers see your collaborative skills. Always be transparent about your work hours and availability.

If you work in a global company, it will be very common to see people replying to emails or engaging in chat conversations in the middle of your nighttime hours because your night might be someone else's daytime. Don't think that you should reply right away. As long as people know your availability and work hours, this shouldn't be a problem. Setting the right expectations regarding availability helps everyone stay productive and understand each other's boundaries.

Summary

In this chapter, you learned about the growth of remote workers and how companies are embracing this model. You also learned about the hybrid work model, where companies ask employees to physically go to the office for part of the week while working remotely the rest of the week. You also learned about how to make an impact as a remote employee—influencing others, actively looking for feedback, staying active, and being transparent. In the next chapter, you will learn more about planning your next career move.

9

What's Next in Your Career?

Be not afraid of growing slowly; be afraid only of standing still.

–Chinese Proverb

We live in a world where immediate recognition brings joy, and you can thank social media for that. Many people post pictures on social media platforms and watch to see how many "likes" they receive. This immediate recognition creates an addiction that can lead to expecting immediate responses and recognition at work. They might even demand a promotion just because they delivered a great project that year—and that's not how most corporate environments work.

When you reach a point in your career where you think a promotion is appropriate, you must evaluate if the best move is to consistently deliver high-quality work while building more confidence and experience or if you should risk changing jobs in hopes of finding room to grow. You need to reflect on what's right for you because there is no right or wrong question. It all depends on your current state (where you are in your job journey or overall career), the possibilities available in your current role, and your tolerable risk level. In cybersecurity, there are many opportunities to either keep growing within your role or move up across different teams and roles. This chapter will teach you more about making the right choice and upcoming cybersecurity opportunities.

Moving Up or Moving Laterally?

Before considering your next step, you need to fully understand where you are and where you want to go. Unfortunately, many people focus exclusively on the financial gains to make this decision, and they put aside what they really love doing, what brings fulfillment to them, and even what they are passionate about. If you put all those elements aside and focus only on financial improvement with this potential new career, chances are you will not be happy in this new role. A Japanese term, Ikigai, describes this. Ikigai combines the Japanese words *ikiru*, "to live," and *kai*, "the realization of what one hopes for." When analyzing where you are and where you want to go, you need to be at least able to answer four questions:

- What do you love doing?
- What do you believe you are good at?
- What do you believe the world needs from you?
- What can you do well and get paid for?

 Note

Read more about the importance of Ikigai in business at https://bit.ly/cybercareerch3link30.

Let's say you work for a company with five salary levels (L1 to L5), and for the past two years, you have been a cybersecurity analyst L2 and expect to be promoted to L3 soon. An opportunity to work on a new AI cybersecurity platform is available, and you have the skills to join the team, but the position is an L2 position, making it a lateral move. According to the company's policy, you must spend at least two years delivering successful results before being promoted to L3. What do you do now? Stay in your current role to get the L3 promotion just around the corner, or embrace this new opportunity and stay in L2 for at least two more years (a total of four years in the same level)?

That's not an easy decision, and I won't pretend there is a formula to tell you what to do next. The correct answer is, "It depends!" Think about your Ikigai—your purpose—and where you want to go as a professional and in your life in general. The answer should consider the following points:

- **Your current risk appetite**: Can you afford this long-term investment, knowing you will need to wait at least two more years to get a promotion? If you're not financially stable, you might not be able to afford it. But only you can answer this question.

- **Growth opportunity**: Are you still learning in your current job? Are you still excited about what you do daily? Are you willing to start from scratch and learn about new technologies? If the answer to the first two questions is "no," then chances are it is time to move anyway. Ideally, the answer to the third question will always be "yes" because if you work with cybersecurity, you must constantly learn new technologies.

- **Work environment**: Do you currently work on a team that supports you? Do you like your current team's culture? Do you work for a manager that empowers you? These are important questions because if you answer "yes" to all these questions, you are most likely in a place where you feel happy. But if you answered "no" to these questions—mainly the last one—it is time to move on. The old saying, *employees quitting managers, not jobs*, applies here. Without a good manager, it is hard to grow and be happy.

- **Work-life balance**: Does your current job allow you to have a good work-life balance? Do you feel you can have a good quality of life and still grow in your current job? If the answer to both questions is "no," then there is a big red flag for you, and it is time to leave.

These are reflection questions, and as you think about them, you might realize you have a great work-life balance in your current job and a great manager who empowers you, but there is no more growth opportunity, and you feel stuck because you aren't learning new things. Now what? You will need to decide if you will step outside of this comfortable zone (a good work environment and work-life balance), to invest in something that will bring you more knowledge and growth over time.

In the cybersecurity field, you will need to be in a place that constantly challenges you to learn more because these challenges will make you a better professional. In addition, you also need to evaluate where you want to go in your career. Maybe you are a cybersecurity analyst today, but your ultimate goal is to become a chief security officer (CSO) at some point. So, if this is the case, the question is, which path will help you to move in that direction? Will the new position allow you to learn the skills you need for a CSO position? Maybe it is time to do another self-assessment!

Self-Assessment

You can use a similar self-assessment approach described in Chapter 3, but don't be thinking about tasks and reflections now. Instead, you need to think more about your current state and where you want to go from here. Every movement you make in your career needs to have a purpose, and learning something new is still a good purpose. Moving just because you are not receiving support from your manager might lead you down an emotional road that only considers your current mental state. As a result, you may end up in a new job you're not happy in either.

Instead of acting impulsively because you are frustrated in your current role, reflect on why you are frustrated and what "good" means to you. Don't make moves based solely on your current mental state. Step back, use critical thinking to analyze the situation, and then reflect on the next steps.

The result of this reflection may be that you want to leave your current job. For example, if you didn't get the promotion you wanted, should you quit and go to a different job, or should you take the feedback given by your manager, improve yourself, deliver a stellar job, and then get the promotion? I always prefer to do the latter. When you isolate your emotions and think through the situation, you will find more clarity and a better understanding of what needs to be done.

Your assessment also needs to consider the skills you have and the skills you will need for the role you want to pursue in the future. Let's say you are a cybersecurity administrator, and your main goal is to become a red team penetration tester. Do you have the skills to be a penetration tester right away, or do you need to learn new skills to be a penetration tester? If you need to learn new skills, is it worth having an intermediate job that will allow you to learn some of the necessary skills, or do you believe you can learn by just getting training?

Based on your desired job's requirements, you will be able to list the areas in which you need to improve and the areas that you need to learn from scratch. If you don't see any opportunity to exercise these needed skills in your current job, evaluate whether you can start ramping up in parallel to learning those skills. When I say ramp up in parallel, I truly mean investing time outside work to learn new skills via formal training or self-study.

Evaluating the Options

Sometimes the path between where you are and where you want to be involves taking multiple steps, and your career is no different. If there is a specific cybersecurity role you want, you must ensure you have the necessary skills to pass the interview and get the job. The best option is to take an intermediate job to gain experience and solidify your foundation before applying to your desired role. Let's use the scenario from Figure 9.1.

Figure 9.1 *Bridging the gap between your current job and the desired one*

In this scenario, you have the qualifications and skills to move to one of the three roles shown in the center column of Figure 9.1. But if you know your main goal is to become a penetration tester, the question becomes which of those three positions will enable you to learn skills that will be important when applying for a penetration tester position? In this case, the answer is incident responder professional. Of course, make sure to look at the job description and responsibilities for all these positions because the definition of what a cloud security admin will do in company A might not be the same as company B. I suggest the incident responder (IR) role because an IR professional needs deep incident investigation knowledge, which will force you to look more deeply into logs, network traces, indicators of attacks, and indicators of compromise and learn about different threat detection technologies. These skills will be very useful when you apply for a penetration tester position.

Following are the key advantages of taking an intermediate position before you achieve your desired role compared with self-studying to gain knowledge:

- **Gain experience**: There's nothing like hands-on experience where you learn things by doing them as part of your job. Even if you only spend one year in a role that will boost your knowledge, it is worth it because there are many unique scenarios you can only learn by practicing in a production environment, making it worth the investment.

- **Expand your network**: A corporate career is about what you know and how good your network is. If you can work with other people and expand your network, your career growth will benefit.

- **Resume improvement**: Expanding your resume and adding more cybersecurity roles that cover a broader spectrum is also beneficial. Sometimes, recruiters will look for this broad knowledge to see if you have across-the-board experience, which could make a difference during the initial resume triage process.

While all these considerations are important, sometimes you might apply for a position even if you don't have all the required qualifications. As long as you don't set high expectations, there is nothing wrong with going through the interview process to learn more about what the hiring team is looking for. Again, all these guidelines are things you should consider, but at the end of the day, it is your decision.

Upcoming Cybersecurity Opportunities

When I wrote this chapter in April 2023, artificial intelligence (AI) was booming in the corporate environment with ChatGPT to facilitate a lot of work—building automations, integrating with products like Microsoft Sentinel, and investigating security-related incidents. In March 2023, Goldman Sachs released an economic research project, "The Potentially Large Effects of Artificial Intelligence on Economic Growth," which estimated about 300 million jobs could be affected by generative AI. While many jobs will be affected, cybersecurity jobs are still on the rise and will benefit from AI.

 Note

You can review the entire report at http://bit.ly/cybercareerch3link31.

In March 2023, Microsoft released the public preview of its first AI-based security tool, Microsoft Security Copilot. This tool can help with incident response, threat hunting, and reporting. All demos from this tool were so impressive that many cybersecurity professionals I know contacted me, expressing their concerns about this tool taking their job. While I empathize with their concerns, I believe this is just another time to adapt to a new reality and use our uniqueness to continue moving forward. The value humans bring to cybersecurity is not replaceable, mainly because we carry unique skills and attitudes that machines can't replace (at least not in the foreseeable future). Remember, it's not only about finding the root cause of an incident. It's about

- Ensuring all stakeholders are aware of what is happening

- Leveraging your soft skills to communicate with the board

- Rationalizing the next investigation step

- Deciding how to move forward based on data and situational awareness of the consequences

- Leading meetings and coming up with a common agreement in a cross-team collaboration

- Many other things that require human interaction

Don't be AI hesitant; be an enabler, a facilitator who will best use this technology to improve overall security. Use this moment to learn something new, see how you can make more impact, and continue to grow.

The market is starting to open AI cybersecurity–specific positions, and when you look at the prerequisites section, you will often see a mix of cybersecurity skills, cloud-native platform, development, and soft skills. Let's use the position shown in Figure 9.2 as an example.

As you can see, the first skill on the list is cybersecurity fundamentals. If you have followed the plan presented in this book, you will have this covered. The next two bullets are about skills not directly related to cybersecurity but that will become critical in this new reality of working with AI: coding and data science skills. If you are a cybersecurity professional who likes coding and dealing with data, this will be a great area to continue investing time to improve. There will be many opportunities like this in the future, and if you are passionate about these fields, go for it.

Artificial Intelligence and Cybersecurity Researcher

★★★★☆ 218 reviews ☑

Full-time

You must create an Indeed account before continuing to the company website to apply

Apply on company site ☑   ⊘

Job details

This role can be performed onsite, remotely, or a hybrid of the two.
Position Requirements
To be considered, you should meet most of the following criteria:

- Knowledge of cybersecurity fundamentals (e.g., access controls, encryption, common software vulnerabilities, and best practices)
- Experience writing object-oriented Python programs including unit testing and version control tools.
- Experience with common data science and machine learning-related Python libraries (e.g., Pandas, Scikit-Learn, Keras).
- Experience using and administering Linux systems.
- Experience using Docker to develop containerized applications.
- Familiarity with common AI paradigms (e.g., Supervised/Unsupervised Learning, Reinforcement Learning, Federated Learning)
- Experience or willingness to learn research-related skills (literature reviews, experiment design, publishing in peer-reviewed venues)
- Skilled at effectively collaborating with both technical and non-technical partners and stakeholders.
- Skilled at sharing knowledge through partnering with and mentoring team members.
- Skilled at oral and written technical communication.
- Experience in a critical infrastructure sector, such as energy distribution is a plus.
- Experience using cognitive architectures such as ACT-R or Soar is a plus.

Figure 9.2 *New AI-related positions opening in the cybersecurity field*

While some positions clearly state the minimum required skills, others may only state the role's responsibilities, as shown in Figure 9.3.

This is a super-interesting position because the job title is Senior Engineer–AI Security Engineer, but there are only two bullets (out of nine) that explicitly call out "security" or "secure". Does that mean you don't need to have a good cybersecurity foundation? No. Remember, having a good cybersecurity foundation is an implicit requirement for any cybersecurity position, mainly if the position is senior level. Another important point of this position is the clear need for broad knowledge, ranging from AI to containers. When working with AI, you will need to bring more value as a professional, which means knowing more things since the AI will be doing the foundational work. That's why I say AI will be a tool to facilitate your work. However, you (the cybersecurity professional) will need to bring more value (knowledge) in different areas.

Senior Engineer - Artificial Intelligence Security Engineer

r

You must create an Indeed account before continuing to the company website to apply

Apply on company site ☑   ⊘

Key Responsibilities

- Implement secure model development life cycle practices with automated white box and black box assessments for AI/ML models.
- Deliver and integrate AI robustness, vulnerability, and stress testing capabilities with Machine Learning Operations ecosystems.
- Evaluate and assess open-source AI security libraries to build into enterprise AI stress testing and audit capabilities.
- Implement end-to-end LLM security risk management processes and automated protections.
- Incorporate machine learning models into diverse application security tooling and processes.
- Support production deployments of AI/ML safety systems using cloud-native packaging and deployment techniques such as containers, serverless, CI/CD and APIs.
- Establish and govern AI/ML and Generative AI application security standards.
- Provide production support and operations for AI/ML security systems.
- Manage cloud deployments and automation frameworks in cloud for AI/ML security systems.

Figure 9.3 *Responsibilities of an AI-related position in the cybersecurity field*

But not everything with embedded AI will require those skills. As I wrote this book, a principal product manager position for Microsoft Security Copilot opened on the customer experience team, which helps bridge the gap between customer insights and engineering/development. The minimum qualifications for the position are shown in Figure 9-4.

Qualifications

Required/Minimum Qualifications:
- Bachelor's Degree AND 8+ years experience in product/service/project/program management or software development
    - OR equivalent experience.

- 3+ years of experience in a technical role in the area of Security Operations, Threat Intelligence, Cyber Incident Response, or Penetration Testing/Red Teaming.
- Advanced knowledge of operating system internals and security mechanisms.
- Experience analyzing attacker techniques.
- Skilled working with extremely large data sets, using tools and scripting languages such as: Excel, KQL, Python, Splunk, and PowerBI.
- Knowledge of kill-chain model, ATT&CK framework, and modern penetration testing techniques.
- Ability to meet Microsoft, customer, and/or government security screening requirements is required for this role. Microsoft Cloud Background Check: This position will be required to pass the Microsoft Cloud background check upon hire/transfer and every two years thereafter.

Figure 9.4 *Product Management position for AI-related technology*

You can see in the first bullet a critical requirement of 3+ years of experience in security operations, threat intelligence, cyber incident response, or penetration testing. This is not an entry-level position that you would apply for after only one year of working with cybersecurity (hence, it's a principal level—higher than senior-level—position. This position also shows that having a deep knowledge of cybersecurity will also enable you to work with AI-related technologies because your deep knowledge of cybersecurity will be extremely helpful in improving this AI experience.

Keep Moving Forward

Congratulations on making it to this point in the book. You now have a roadmap of what you need to do and how you should approach your switch to the cybersecurity field. It is important to mention that you will often doubt yourself throughout this journey. You might even have to deal with imposter syndrome. Keep pushing yourself. Put yourself in scenarios that challenge you to learn more and do more.

Make sure to have short-, mid-, and long-term goals to keep you engaged and accountable for your progress. While progress is important, you also need to understand that improvement takes time, and not moving up—or even laterally—after two years in the same role doesn't mean you are failing. If you are learning and growing in your profession, you are not failing; you are getting better. Don't measure your improvement solely based on your promotions. You need to think broadly about how you are growing and always consider your level of happiness doing what you are doing.

While we close this chapter with the end of your cybersecurity career roadmap, the next chapter will open your mind to another possibility: becoming a cybersecurity entrepreneur.

Summary

This chapter taught you what's next in your career and what you need to consider when planning your career movement. You learned about moving up or laterally. You also learned about the upcoming opportunities in cybersecurity, including the addition of AI to the cybersecurity field. In the next chapter, you will learn more about what it takes to build your own cybersecurity business.

10

Owning a Cybersecurity Business

I knew that if I failed, I wouldn't regret that, but I knew the one thing I might regret is not trying.

–Jeff Bezos

Fear of failure prevents potential business owners from ever realizing their dreams. For cybersecurity professionals, fear of failure leads to fear of ever even trying — limiting your professional growth.

Once you've gained some experience in cybersecurity — and if you already have an entrepreneurial spirit — you may feel enticed to open your own business and provide your services to many customers. Many cybersecurity opportunities are available for contractors, consultants, and business owners because the market needs specialized services. You should always feel empowered to pursue these areas if you have the skills and knowledge to benefit multiple customers. But what else does it take to fly solo in this competitive market? In this chapter, you will learn more insights about what it takes to open your cybersecurity business from the perspective of two business owners — Paula Januszkiewicz and David Kennedy —who are guest authors for this chapter.

Knowing More about the Guest Authors

When I was planning this book and writing the table of contents, I wanted to incorporate an entrepreneurial perspective from someone who's both a company owner and a successful cybersecurity professional.

I've known Paula Januszkiewicz (see Figure 10.1) for more than 10 years through her close relationship with Microsoft; we've attended and presented at many conferences. Paula is the Founder and CEO of CQURE Academy and CQURE, which she established in 2008. She is also an enterprise security MVP, honorable Microsoft regional director, and a world-class cybersecurity expert, consulting with customers worldwide. In 2017, Paula graduated from Harvard Business School. She delivers keynotes and presentations at the biggest world conferences such RSA, Black Hat, Microsoft Ignite, SecTor Canada, AISA, GISEC, GITEX, LEAP, and many others. She is often a top-rated speaker, including being a number one speaker at Microsoft Ignite (among 1,100 speakers at a conference with 26,000 attendees) and Black Hat Asia 2019, also an RSA conference, where her two sessions were among the top five. Paula is known for her unique stage presence that is always well-received among diverse audiences, often gathering thousands of people.

Paula has more than 19 years of experience in cybersecurity, performing penetration tests, architecture consulting, training, and seminars. She takes more than 200 flights annually to provide cybersecurity services for CQURE's customers. She and her team create security awareness programs for various organizations and their top management. They create various security tools (CQTools) supporting penetration tests, incident response, and forensics. Paula is a technical advisory board member at the Royal Bank of Scotland/Natwest.

Figure 10.1 *Paula and Yuri at TechEd North America 2013*

Although I met my friend David Kennedy (see Figure 10.2) on Twitter through our shared passion for fitness, I already knew him through his reputation in the cybersecurity industry. David started the *We Hack Health* podcast and founded Binary Defense and TrustedSec, focusing on improving the security industry. David is the former chief security officer (CSO) of Diebold Incorporated, where he ran both physical and information security on a global scale. David served on the ISC2 board of directors for several years.

Figure 10.2 *Yuri and David on the Overcome podcast in 2023*

David co-authored "Metasploit: The Penetration Testers Guide" and created the Social-Engineer Toolkit (SET), Artillery, Unicorn, PenTesters Framework, and several popular open-source tools. David is relied upon frequently as a subject matter expert, has testified in front of Congress numerous times, helped drive new cybersecurity policy, and is frequently called as an expert on major news outlets. David has presented at some of the world's largest cybersecurity conferences and thousands of presentations worldwide. David served as a technical adviser and was featured on the *Mr. Robot* television show. David is one of the founding authors of the Penetration Testing Execution Standard (PTES), a framework designed to fix the penetration testing industry. David co-founded DerbyCon, a large-scale conference started in Louisville, Kentucky. Before moving to the private sector, David worked for the United States Marine Corps and was deployed to Iraq twice and additional Mideast countries for intelligence-related missions.

Stepping Stones to Flying Solo

If you are reading this book and are still transitioning to cybersecurity, flying solo and building your own business might not even be what you want for your future. Even if that's the case, you should feel empowered to read the testimonies of the two guest authors for this chapter. However, if you have plans or a long-term vision for a cybersecurity business, this chapter is even more important because it provides best practices from cybersecurity professionals who became business owners.

When it comes to the cybersecurity business, particularly if you start as a consultant, you will see many options for providing services to customers. You can have a broad portfolio of options that covers the entire end-to-end experience in cybersecurity, or you can focus on providing specialized services that only cover a specific scope. Both options are feasible if you can assemble a good team, because it will be hard to do everything independently.

Whether you offer a broad range of services or a more specialized one depends on several factors. For example, you may not have the initial capital to hire more people, and you don't have the skills to cover too many services, so you can start creating an offering that takes advantage of your skills and cover only the services you feel comfortable designing and implementing. With time, and as the money starts to flow, you may re-think adding more services and hiring people to perform them. One service that always has good demand is penetration testing. This type of service usually includes performing the penetration test based on the scope of resources agreed to in the contract and might include a vulnerability assessment. A report shows the penetration test report and recommendations for improving security.

On the other hand, more areas can be covered with a broader portfolio. For example, suppose you advertise that your company specializes in architecting end-to-end cybersecurity solutions for hybrid environments (on-premises and cloud). In that case, you will be responsible for designing the entire solution, from secure client access to cloud workload protection. This type of project can take months to finish and will likely require multiple people to cover all the areas.

That's why it is important to have clarity when building your cybersecurity business. Make sure you can answer the following questions before you start:

- What type of service do you want to offer?

  - Make sure to be very precise in your portfolio to set the correct expectation. There is a natural temptation to say, "We do everything related to cybersecurity," but if you start with this slogan and can't deliver, you will hurt your brand and business.

- Who is your target audience?

  - Are you going to target small, medium, or large organizations? If you are starting a business without a team to help you, this is a very important consideration. If you initially target large organizations and cannot deliver, this can and will hurt your brand. Be realistic and make sure you can deliver on your promises.

Now that you have this foundational knowledge, read the testimonials from Paula Januszkiewicz and David Kennedy about their cybersecurity entrepreneur journeys.

Paula Januszkiewicz's Keys to Entrepreneurial Success

If you want to make it in the world of cybersecurity, you had better learn to love change, hard work, teamwork, and risk. Everything is evolving at lightning speed: Hackers are getting smarter because cybercrime is a lucrative business, and there are still not enough experts in the field. Sure, cybercriminals have been here almost since the beginning of time, but now is their golden age. So, it is no surprise that getting into cybersecurity now is an even better opportunity than when I started my own company in 2008, although staying on top of the growing competition and keeping your knowledge up to date can sometimes be quite challenging.

At first, I was the only one. Back then, CQURE was just a small cybersecurity consultancy, mainly performing penetration tests, presentations, and client training, but over the last 15 years, my company has steadily grown to employ nearly 50 people, delivering services to organizations all over the globe. After all these years, I feel quite proud of my achievements, but there is no one-size-fits-all recipe for success in this field. But based on my own experiences, I have some advice that could help you grow — whether you're a fresh-faced entrepreneur starting your first business or a seasoned pro with a wealth of experience. Here is the kicker: These tips relate to your personal and professional life because I believe you cannot be a great cybersecurity entrepreneur without a healthy balance.

Key Elements for Success

When I started my entrepreneurial journey, I quickly realized that success was not only about having a great product or service; it was also about setting clear objectives and priorities, committing them with unwavering determination, and simply doing what I loved. Knowing where I wanted to go and why was like having a roadmap guiding me toward my destination. When you have a passion for your work, your enthusiasm becomes contagious, and others will notice. Whether leading a team or working solo, being committed to your goals and sharing your passion can help you achieve more than you ever thought possible. In cybersecurity, this is perhaps even more important than in other fields because, without genuine interest and commitment, it's easy to fall behind and feel dissatisfied.

Having a drive is probably equally crucial. It's the kind of motivation that gets you up in the morning, ready to take on the day and eager to learn something new. My drive has always been about expanding my knowledge and staying up to date on the latest trends and developments in the tech world. The abundance of resources available nowadays makes this much easier than before. You can spend hours on GitHub, Twitter, or YouTube, read books and articles available for free, listen to podcasts, watch webinars, or talk with other professionals. I'm always looking for new information and insights, not only to use in my work but also to fuel my ambition.

Another key element of managing a successful business is discipline. Without it, achieving long-term success can be challenging. As a business owner, I understand that discipline is about working hard, staying focused on objectives, and developing a mindset that fosters success. A disciplined mind brings happiness — not just to your professional life but to your entire life. It's a skill that needs to be honed and constantly maintained rather than an innate talent. A disciplined mind requires the right conditions to flourish, which starts with setting priorities and objectives. Once you know what you want to achieve, create a plan and break down tasks into manageable parts. Assign responsibilities to the right people to ensure everyone is working towards the same goals.

Effective organization is also critical to success. A well-organized business is more efficient and productive. Good organization can help entrepreneurs streamline their operations and make more informed decisions, from managing client relationships to keeping track of finances. Again, this is not something you are born with but rather a skill that you painstakingly develop over many years, so if you're a beginner struggling with keeping everything organized, do not worry. We have all been there! Nobody is perfect, but one important component on our path to great organization is acknowledging our mistakes and improving. In other words, do not waste too much time on judgments, especially about yourself. It is important to know what you can do better, and that is it. We are born to move forward — a crucial factor for growth.

And yet, you will find it impossible to move forward without constantly learning. This skill combines your inner drive, discipline, and good organization. You can learn from many sources, and diversification is essential. Stay updated on the latest trends and technologies in your industry. The best way to learn is by doing, so write blogs, articles, or anything that requires you to actively seek out information. Learn from your team, the people you meet, and your clients. Most importantly, learn from your successes and mistakes. Do not let setbacks discourage you — they are inevitable. Embrace them and learn from them. I have had my fair share of failures along the way. In fact, I believe those failures helped me grow and learn the most. So, if you're looking to make it in cybersecurity (or any other field, for that matter), remember to stay curious and disciplined; the rest just comes by itself.

Being open to new challenges is equally essential to personal and professional growth. It can be daunting to try new things, especially if they involve stepping out of your comfort zone. But embracing new challenges can lead to exciting opportunities, new connections, and valuable experiences. In my career, I've had the opportunity to present at some of the biggest conferences in the world, sometimes even giving keynote speeches. It was nerve-wracking at first, but I quickly realized that the more I put myself out there, the more opportunities came my way. Never decline an opportunity simply because it seems difficult, unfamiliar, or uncomfortable. And while it's important to stay focused on your goals and priorities, being open to new challenges can sometimes help you achieve them even faster than you thought possible. So, next time you're presented with a new form of media or a chance to break into a new market, don't hesitate to take it on. Embrace the challenge and see where it takes you.

Giving back to the community is also challenging, but I think it's crucial for success in cybersecurity. It's about supporting community events and sharing knowledge and expertise with others. By doing so, you help professionals and gain respect and recognition in the industry. Throughout my career, I have always tried to give more than I take, which has paid off in numerous ways. I didn't set out to become a Microsoft MVP or RD, but I got those titles by putting in extra effort to help others and build up the community. It is important to be humble and helpful and remember that sometimes the most rewarding experiences come from contributing to an important cause, even if it does not involve monetary compensation. In my experience, those who are willing to give selflessly are often the ones who reap the greatest rewards in the end.

However, the above advice is insufficient to start and run a cybersecurity business successfully. The last key element transcends you as an individual regardless of how disciplined, hard-working, educated, and organized you are. You will not get far without a rock-solid team.

Building a killer team is the name of the game when it comes to running a successful business, and let me tell you, diversity is key. Cybersecurity is not just about mad technical skills; it requires a pinch of creativity and a dash of critical thinking combined with good soul and social skills. So, why not have a team with different backgrounds and perspectives? With a diverse team, you can approach problems from all angles and come up with more creative and innovative solutions. Teamwork makes a difference.

Once you have assembled your dream team, it is crucial to help them grow and unleash their full potential. Every team member has unique strengths, and it is your job as a leader to help them identify and develop them. Whether providing growth opportunities, giving constructive feedback, or investing in training and development programs, you must ensure your team is constantly improving.

But let's be real here. Sometimes, things do not work out, and you have to let go of the dead weight. No matter how hard you try to support and train your team members, sometimes they just aren't the right fit. It's tough, but it's necessary for both the individual and the company to cut the cord. While we're on the topic of teams, let me tell you, animosities between departments are a big no-no. If people don't like each other, it can cause major hiccups in the workflow. So, make sure everyone shares your vision and objectives, and try to create a harmonious work environment where people can work together and help each other out.

Building a team is not easy, and things can get messy sometimes. Just like in cybersecurity, the human element is crucial, and sometimes people just do not click. But with the right leadership and team spirit, you can make it work. So, find yourself a team that shares your values and is willing to work like it's their business, and watch your company soar to new heights! After all these years, I can also say that finding people you can trust is one of the crucial growth factors — for them and yourself. I am sure you are familiar with the approach that good ideas are born when you are at rest, usually on vacation. It works the same way when surrounded by people you can trust. When you stop feeling the pressure, your brain goes somewhere else, and as we all know, creativity is crucial in cybersecurity.

Common Pitfalls and Challenges

In general, running a cybersecurity company can be quite tricky. There are tons of risks, dangers, and challenges that you'll need to deal with along the way. If you're just starting out, one of the biggest challenges will be establishing a solid reputation and finding clients. Convincing potential clients to trust your new company with their sensitive data and security needs can be tough, especially when there's so much competition. That's why it's super important to find a way to differentiate yourself from the crowd and stand out, be it a unique approach, a one-of-a-kind product, or an unmatched team of experts.

But, even if you have been in business for a while, there are still plenty of risks to watch out for. The cybersecurity industry constantly evolves, and new threats and technologies can emerge seemingly out of nowhere. It's tough to keep up with all of these changes, but you need to if you want to ensure that your company's solutions are effective and current. That means investing in research and development and adapting and pivoting as needed.

One major pitfall for seasoned company owners and executives is becoming complacent. It's easy to get overconfident and assume your company's solutions are bulletproof. But that can lead to overlooking potential vulnerabilities and leaving your clients exposed. Plus, as your company grows and becomes more successful, it can become a bigger target for cybercriminals. So, staying vigilant and investing in the latest security measures is important. Otherwise, the hunter might become the prey!

While all these considerations are important, you might feel empowered to apply for a position you lack all the qualifications for. As long as you don't set high expectations, there is nothing wrong with going through the interview process to learn more about what they (the hiring team) are looking for. Again, all these guidelines are things you should consider, but at the end of the day, it is your decision.

It's important to prioritize ongoing education and training for your team to avoid some of these risks. Encourage your employees to attend industry conferences, take courses and certifications, and stay current on the latest trends and threats. Investing in regular security assessments and penetration testing is crucial for identifying potential weaknesses in your company's systems and processes.

It is also super important to be transparent and honest with clients about any potential risks or limitations in your solutions. Don't promise a level of security that you can't deliver. Instead, be clear about what your solutions can and cannot do. Work with clients to find the best approach to meet their unique security needs.

Finally, be honest with yourself and others. Do not be afraid that your knowledge is incomplete; you can always learn. Do not be afraid to admit you made a mistake; you can always do things better. Cybersecurity is a very demanding market, and there are arrogant people everywhere who want to discredit things you do. If you believe in what you do and do it right, just ignore them, live your proud life, and bring the change.

David Kennedy: Starting from the Ground Up

Are you worried that you don't know how to start a business and be successful? Neither did I. In 2011, I was one of the youngest vice presidents and chief security officers in the history of the Fortune 1000 company I worked for, and I wondered what was next. I had built a great team, a global international cybersecurity program that tackled the risks for our business, and I was highly successful at it. I had an amazing team, no worries about losing my job, and buy-in for any security project I wanted to accomplish. This is the pinnacle of what most in our industry dream of — security integrated into the business, respect, and always pushing the envelope at high speed. The board of directors loved us, and our executives were supportive. We had everything. Yet, I went home at night wondering what was next.

In late 2011, I was making the hour-long drive home from Canton, Ohio, to Middleburg Heights. This drive gave me a lot of time to reflect, think about various topics, and most importantly, unwind after a long day. I wondered what was next. I wanted to start my own company but had no idea how to do it. What if I failed? How do I even start a company? How will I be successful? A whirlwind of emotions surrounded me on the way home. My wife recently had twins, and our three kids were all very young. Was now the right time? What if I fail? How will I support my family?

After discussing the idea with my partner, Erin, we both agreed we needed to pursue starting my own company because we would never have an opportunity to do it again. I had never started a business before, so I had no idea how to do any of this other than my experiences in a small startup and my time at a Fortune 1000 company. All I knew was that I believed in myself and that it would be successful if I focused all my mind and effort on this and my family. Erin started taking finance classes at night to learn accounting software and keep the books while I started putting together a website, proposals, and sales material and testing the market by calling my industry contacts.

My idea was to start a small consulting business first because it didn't require a ton of upfront capital and was something I could scale up or down depending on how well it was doing. I also wanted to stay clear of venture capital and private equity money to focus on my culture and vision while maintaining control of the company. I had an ultimate vision of starting an additional company, but this would come later when I had the funds and investments to do it. In July 2012, I opened the doors to TrustedSec in the basement of my house with two employees — Erin and me. The biggest advice I can ever give everyone looking to start a successful business is to believe in yourself. Erin was instrumental in our early and continued success, so if you can rope in your partner, it's a great thing.

If you are already successful in what you do, what makes you think you won't be successful at something new? It'll be hard, and you'll spend countless hours frustrated or scared, but you'll pull through stronger each time. In our first year, we had three employees, but we now have more than 150 employees worldwide. I started a second company (my ultimate vision) called Binary Defense (BD) with more than 200 employees worldwide. Building something you believe in can help others and help you stay true to those principles and values. Don't do something different because another company does it a certain way. Focus on what makes you unique and forge the company, its culture, and the people you surround yourself with to build on success.

One of the biggest challenges I see younger companies face is the inability of the founder or leaders to step away from their roles and responsibilities when necessary and pass them on to other company leaders. It won't always be just you. You will need to rely on others. Also, remember that hiring someone to take on some of your responsibility will make you even busier temporarily, but it will eventually reduce your workload.

My early successes with TrustedSec and BD helped build my reputation, persona, credibility, and ultimately, the companies I started. Your company must represent your persona and credibility in the industry — which means being able to perform at a high level that matches what you've built. When you come to TrustedSec or BD, you can assume excellence in every aspect of the business and a culture that believes in our mission to make the world safer. As you expand into different services, ensure you have the experience to perform that work at a high level. It doesn't mean there won't be bumps in the road, but you must identify which security service fits your portfolio and how to monitor it.

Following are five principles that helped Dave Kennedy be successful and create successful businesses:

- **Credibility**: Continue to build your reputation by contributing to the industry to improve it and never fail to do the right thing.

- **Learning**: Know that you can't possibly know everything and that you will learn whatever you need to know when it becomes important for you to learn it. Learn every day.

- **Improving**: Focus on what you have and always strive to improve it, even if it's already the best in the industry.

- **Customer Success**: Your success single-handedly relies on your ability to deliver for your customers. Develop customer relationships, help them, and never fret about working overtime or doing something extra if it's right for them.

- **People**: People make up your company and your culture. Hire people that believe in your mission for success. You will make mistakes. You can't always make the perfect hire 100 percent of the time. Find people who care for the company, and take care of the people who work for you. In return, the same will happen.

Starting your own business might seem overwhelming and impossible. It's not. Anyone can do it; if you believe in yourself, anything is possible. It might not succeed the first time. It might take a few tries, but you'll get there and be happier that you took a plunge instead of just thinking about it. The rewards are endless, as is the happiness of doing your own thing.

Final Considerations

As we come to the end of this chapter, I hope that you have found the advice and stories helpful and insightful. Remember that entrepreneurship in cybersecurity is not an easy road, but it can be extremely rewarding. Take the time to educate yourself about the industry, network with other professionals, and constantly work to improve your skills and your business. Do not be afraid to take risks, but always be aware of the potential dangers and take steps to protect yourself and your company.

In the future, the cybersecurity industry will continue to evolve and adapt to new threats and challenges. Stay informed and be prepared to adapt along with it. Always remember that while running a business can be a rollercoaster ride, the ultimate reward is the ability to create something that can make a difference in the world. So, stay optimistic, dedicated, and focused on your goals. The future is bright, and with the right mindset and skills, you can succeed in cybersecurity entrepreneurship.

I want to leave you with one of my favorite quotes that has driven me for many years. Neil Gaiman said: "You get work however you get work. But you keep working because your work is good, you're easy to get along with, and you deliver the work on time. And you don't even need all three. Two out of three is fine."

Of course, you should strive for perfection and try to tick all three boxes, but bear in mind that if you always keep up the good work, sometimes it is okay to choose from the remaining two. Good luck!

Summary

Building your own business is not an easy task. Building a cybersecurity business that will face stiff competition might be even harder, but the market is vast, and there is a need for good cybersecurity professionals who can offer quality service. While this chapter may not be for everyone, it includes important tips that can enlighten your long-term vision about where you want to go in this field and help you understand the possibilities. In this chapter, you learned about making an initial assessment of pursuing a solo cybersecurity career, the keys to entrepreneurial success, and considerations for starting your cybersecurity business.

Index

Numerics

20 Coolest Careers in Cybersecurity, 8–9

A

active listening, 133
adjusting your cybersecurity skills, 117–119
AI (artificial intelligence), 112
  ChatGPT, 144
  Microsoft Security Copilot, 145
  -related skills, 145–148
Amazon, hybrid work environment, 130
Angelou, M., 133
application security, 6
attacks, simulating in the lab, 57–58
automation, vulnerability assessment, 104
Azure Security Center in the Field, 135–136

B

Bezos, J., 119
bias
  confirmation, 116
  implicit, 115–116
  reducing, 116–117
big tech, cybersecurity jobs in, 19–20
Binary Defense, 158–159
"Bitwarden password vaults targeted in Google ads phishing attack", 26
blogs, 52
  Rapid7's impact by OpenSSL Buffer Overflow Vulnerability, 29
  Scripting Guy, 73
blue team, 7, 58
BSides, 66
buffer overflow, 29
burnout, 121
BYOD (bring your own device), 68, 73

C

calligraphy, 108
career/s. *See also* job/s
  being passionate about, 8, 22–23, 62–63, 154
  changing, 3–4, 47, 71
  cybersecurity, 4, 22
    job requirements, 9–12
    job titles, 8–10
  planning
    evaluating the options, 143–144
    explore your current skill, 26–30
    organizing your plan, 32–34
    self-assessment, 142–143
    SMART Goals, 30–32
    upcoming opportunities, 144–148
CC (Certified in Cybersecurity), 37
CCT (Certified Cybersecurity Technician), 41–42

CEH (Certified Ethical Hacker), 39
certification, 34
  CCT (Certified Cybersecurity Technician), 41–42
  CISSP, 37
  versus college degree, 35
  CompTIA CySA+, 40–41
  CompTIA Security+, 35, 38–39
  Cyber and IT Security Foundation certification, 37–38
  ECSS (EC-Council Certified Security Specialist), 39–40
  ISACA (Information Systems Auditing & Control Association), 36
  MCP (Microsoft Certified Professional), 35
  specializations, 42–43
  SSCP (Systems Security Certified Practitioner), 41
  vendor-specific, 43–44
changing careers, 3–4, 47
chat, 131
ChatGPT, 144
cloud security
  architecture, 6
  multi-, 57
  posture management, 56
coachability, 15
Cobalt Strike, 46
collaboration, 15–16, 107, 134
commands, ipconfig, 60
communication/communicating
  bad news, 107–108
  influencing others, 132–133
  remote worker, 131
  skills, 39
compliance, regulatory, 57
CompTIA
  CySA+ certification, 40–41
  Newsletter, 30
  Security+ certification, 35, 38–39
Conficker, 101
confirmation bias, 116
consulting, 152–153, 158

continuing education, 157
COVID-19 pandemic, 128, 135
CQURE/CQURE Academy, 150, 153–154
Cracking the PM Interview, 21
creative thinking, 107, 134–135
critical thinking, 15
CSO (chief security officer), 5
curiosity, 155
Cyber Seek Heatmap, 17–19
cybersecurity, 4, 17–19
  analyst, 9
  bias
    confirmation, 116
    implicit, 115–116
    reducing, 116–117
  careers, 4
  certification. See certification
  consulting, 152–153, 158
  diversity, 100–101
  job/s, 8–12
    basic qualifications, 10
    in big tech, 19–20
    marketing, 21
    product development, 21
    product engineering, 21
    product support, 21
    requirements, 9–12
    research, 21
    responsibilities and expectations, 103–104
    tenure, 12
    titles, 8–10
  obstacles, 112–114
  penetration testing, 152
  professionals, 100
  roles and responsibilities, 5–8
  running a business
    common pitfalls and challenges, 156–157
    key elements for success, 154–156
  skills
    adjusting, 117–119
    assessment, 26–30
    interviewing, 11–12
    soft, 14–17
    technical, 12–14

specializations, 5–8, 42–43
terminology, 27
threat intelligence, 6
WLB (work-life balance). See WLB (work-life balance)
workforce gap, 4
Cybersecurity Workforce Study 2022, 4

D

daily tasks, 124–125
dashboards, 108
data security, 6
Deep Instinct, "Voice of SecOps Report 2022", 112–113
delegation, 16, 107
DevOps, 6
diet and exercise, 122
Diogenes, Y.
  Azure Security Center in the Field, 135–136
  Enterprise Mobility Suite Managing BYOD and Company-Owned Devices, 73
  Overcome podcast, 112, 121
  Ready, Set, Achieve!: A Guide to Taking Charge of Your Life Creating Balance, and Achieving Your Goals, 30, 120
  Windows Server 2012 Security from End to Edge and Beyond: Architecting, Designing, Planning, and Deploying Windows Server 2012 Security Solutions, 72
direct questions, 92
directory services, 28
discipline, 154
discovery phase, threat intelligence, 60
diversity, 100–101
DMZ (demilitarized zone), 28
DNS (Domain Name Service), query filter, 53

E

EC-Council University Cyber Talks, 67, 68–69
ECSS (EC-Council Certified Security Specialist), 39–40
email, 131
empathy, 15, 133
employer, treating as your customer, 106–108
From End to Edge and Beyond, 72
endpoint security, 7
enthusiasm, 87
entrepreneur mindset, 106–108. *See also* success, key
elements for
ethical hacker, 100
exercise, physical, 122
Exin, Cyber and IT Security Foundation certification, 37–38

F

fear of failure, 140
feedback
    employee, 133
    manager, 104
    soliciting, 133–134
feelings
    gratitude, 114
    not taking things personally, 114–115
    stoicism, 113–114
filter
    DNS query, 53
    job search, 80–81
"Flexera 2022 State of the Cloud Report", 57
formal interview rounds, 88

G

Gaiman, N., 160
Gilbert, J., *Enterprise Mobility Suite Managing BYOD and Company-Owned Devices*, 73
Glassdoor.com, 19

Global Workplace Analytics, 128–129
gratitude, 114
growth mindset, 15

H

Hackers for Change, 70
Heuer, R. J., *Psychology of Intelligence Analysis*, 116
HIPAA (Health Insurance Portability and Accountability Act), 57
Holiday, R., *The Obstacle Is the Way: The Timeless Art of Turning Trials into Triumph*, 112
hybrid work, 130

I

IKE (Internet Key Exchange), 28
Ikigai, 140
implicit bias, 115–116
incident response, 120
inclusivity, 15
Information System Security Association International, 67
infrastructure and endpoint security, 7
interviewing, 11–12, 16–17, 66
    final decision, 93
    formal rounds, 88
    initial triage, 27
    interviewer angles, 88–89
    making a good impression, 86–87
    note-taking, 90
    power of enthusiasm, 87
    preparation, 85–87
    pre-triage process, 84
    questions, 90
        about previous experience, 92–93
        direct, 92
        fictitious scenario, 93
        scenario-based, 91
        technical, 88–89
IP (Internet Protocol), 54
ipconfig command, 60

IPsec, 28
ISACA (Information Systems Auditing & Control Association), cybersecurity fundamentals certification, 36
ISC2 (International Information System Security Certification Consortium)
    CISSP certification, 37
    SSCP certification, 41

J

Januszkiewicz, P., 150, 153–154
job/s, 8–12, 27. *See also* interviewing; planning, career; remote work/er
    advancement/promotion, 119, 140, 142–143
        considerations, 141–142
        Ikigai, 140
        intermediate position, 143–144
        upcoming opportunities, 144–148
    competencies, 88
    cybersecurity
        basic qualifications, 10
        big tech, 19–20
        mapping your responsibilities, 104–105
        marketing, 21
        obstacles, 112–114
        product development, 21
        product engineering, 21
        product support, 21
        requirements, 9–12
        research, 21
        responsibilities and expectations, 103–104
        stress, 113
        tenure, 12
        titles, 8–12
    interviewing, 11–12, 16–17, 66. *See also* interviewing
        final decision, 93
        initial triage, 85
        making a good impression, 86–87

power of enthusiasm, 87
preparation, 85–87
pre-triage process, 84
lateral movement, 103
searching. See also
network/ing
Cyber Seek Heatmap,
17–19
LinkedIn, 79–81
phases, 94–95
progress timeline, 77–78
updating your resume,
78–79
Jobs, S., 8, 63, 108
Journal of Applied
Psychology, 8

K-L

Kennedy, D., 121, 151, 158–160
"Metasploit: The
Penetration Testers
Guide", 152
lab
creating, 49
open-source, 46
operating systems process,
49–52
requirements, 46–49
scenarios
attack simulation, 57–58
cloud security posture
management, 56
multi-cloud security, 57
network traffic analysis,
52–55
regulatory compliance, 57
self-assessment, 60–62
SIEM (security
information and event
management), 58–59
threat hunting, 59
threat intelligence, 59–60
Windows Process
Monitor, 50–52
lateral movement, 103
leadership, 107
leveraging your skills,
108–109
LinkedIn, 9, 74–75, 79–81, 123
Linux, attack simulation, 58
listening, active, 133

M

MAC (Media Access Control)
address, 54
manager, feedback, 104
mapping your responsibilities,
104–105
marketing, 21
master's degree, 72–73
MCP (Microsoft Certified
Professional), 35
meetings, online, 131, 132
mental health, WLB (work-life
balance), 121, 123
Meta, 129
Microsoft Defender for Cloud,
56, 57, 135–136
Microsoft Outlook, tasks,
124–125
Microsoft Planner, 32–34
Microsoft Security Copilot, 145
Microsoft Sentinel, 58–59
Miller, J., *Ready, Set, Achieve!:*
A Guide to Taking Charge of
Your Life Creating Balance,
and Achieving Your
Goals, 30
mindset
entrepreneur, 106–108
of not taking things
personally, 114–115
MITRE ATT&CK
framework, 60
motivation, 154
multi-cloud security, 57

N

network/ing, 66. *See also*
interviewing
finding inward
opportunities, 70–71
online events and
communities, 67, 69–70
online presence, 73–74
LinkedIn, 74–75
Twitter, 76–77
security, 5
forensics, 52
traffic analysis, 52–55
VPN (virtual private
network), 27–28

security conferences,
66–67, 68–69
volunteering, 70, 71
newsletter, CompTIA, 30
NIST (National Institute of
Standards and Technology), 38
note-taking
interview, 90
post-deployment, 106

O

online events and
communities, 67
online meetings, 131, 132
online presence, 73–74
LinkedIn, 74–75
perception, 137
Twitter, 76–77
YouTube, 75–76
open-source lab, 46
operating systems
Linux, attack simulation, 58
Windows
attack simulation, 58
Process Monitor, 50–52
operational hygiene, 104
organizational structure, 102–103
Overcome podcast, 112
overthinking, 71
Ozkaya, E., 68

P

penetration testing, 152
physical exercise, 122
planning, career. *See also*
network/ing
evaluating the options,
143–144
explore your current skill,
26–30
Ikigai, 140
organizing your plan, 32–34
overthinking, 71
ramp-up phase, 105
self-assessment, 142–143
SMART Goals, 30–32
upcoming opportunities,
144–148
PoC (Proof of Concept), 106
podcasts

Overcome, 112, 121
We Hack Health, 121
posture management, 7
"The Potentially Large Effects
    of Artificial Intelligence on
    Economic Growth", 144
preparing for an interview,
    85–87
problem-solving skills, 133
Process Monitor, 50–52
processes, 50–51
product development, 21
product engineering, 21
product management, 19
product support, 21
promotion
    considerations, 141–142
    Ikigai, 140
    self-assessment, 142–143
PTES (Penetration Testing
    Execution Standard), 152

Q

questions, interview, 90
    about previous experience,
        92–93
    direct, 92
    fictitious scenario, 93
    scenario-based, 91

R

ramp-up phase, 105
*Rapid7's impact by OpenSSL
    Buffer Overflow
    Vulnerability*, 29
red team, 7, 58
reducing bias, 116–117
regulatory compliance, 57
remote work/er, 128
    creativity, 134–135
    growth of, 128–129
    influencing others,
        132–133
    online communication, 131
    soliciting feedback,
        133–134
    time management, 135
    transparency, 136–137

report, lab scenario, 49
requirements, lab, 46–49
research, 21, 85–86
responsibilities
    adjusting, 117–119
    cybersecurity job,
        103–104
    mapping, 104–105
resume, 11–12
    certification versus college
        degree, 35
    updating, 78–79
Robertson, D., *How to Think
    Like a Roman Emperor: The
    Stoic Philosophy of Marcus
    Arelius*, 112
roles and responsibilities,
    cybersecurity, 5–8
RTO (return-to-office)
    mandate, 130

S

scenario-based questions, 91
scenarios, lab, 46–49
    attack simulation, 57–58
    cloud security posture
        management, 56
    multi-cloud security, 57
    network traffic analysis,
        52–55
    operating systems process,
        49–52
    regulatory compliance, 57
    self-assessment, 60–62
    SIEM (security information
        and event management),
        58–59
    threat hunting, 59
    threat intelligence, 59–60
Scripting Guy blog, 73
security conferences, 66–67
self-assessment
    career advancement,
        142–143
    lab, 60–62
    technical skills, 12–14
Seneca, 113–114
Senior Engineer–AI Security
    Engineer, 146

Shinder, T., *Windows Server
    2012 Security from End
    to Edge and Beyond:
    Architecting, Designing,
    Planning, and Deploying
    Windows Server 2012
    Security Solutions*, 72
SIEM (security information
    and event management), 46,
    58–59
skills
    adjusting, 117–119
    AI-related, 145–148
    assessment, 26–30, 142–143
    communication, 39, 133
    critical thinking, 15
    interviewing, 11–12
    leveraging, 108–109
    mapping your
        responsibilities, 104–105
    organization, 154–155
    problem-solving, 133
    soft, 14–17, 84
    technical, 12–14, 84
sleep, 123
SMART Goals, 30–32, 114
SOC (security operations
    center), 6, 59, 112
soft skills, 14–17, 84
specializations
    certification, 42–43
    cybersecurity, 5–8
    penetration testing, 152
SSCP (Systems Security
    Certified Practitioner)
    certification, 41
State of Remote Work 2020, 128
stoicism, 112, 113–115
stress, 113, 118–119, 135
success, key elements for, 154,
    159–160
    curiosity, 155
    discipline, 154
    facing challenges, 155
    giving back to the
        community, 155
    motivation, 154
    organization, 154–155
    teamwork, 156
Swider, B., 86

T

tasks
  daily, 124–125
  plan-creation exercise,
    105–106
teams and teamwork
  diversity, 100–101
  lateral movement, 103
  organizational structure,
    102–103
  success and, 156
  virtual, 114
technical skills, 12–14, 84
technical writing, 72
terminology, 27
threads, 51
threat hunting, 59
threat intelligence, 6, 59–60
  discovery phase, 60
  MITRE ATT&CK
    framework, 60
time management
  daily tasks, 124–125
  recommendations, 125
  remote worker, 135
  weekly goals, 124
tools
  communication, 131
  Cyber Seek Heatmap, 17–19

  lab, 47–48
  Microsoft Planner, 32–34
  Wireshark, network traffic
    analysis, 52–55
training, 157
transparency, 136–137, 157
TrustedSec, 121, 158
tunnel vision, 120
Twitter, 76–77, 151

U

UDP (User Datagram
  Protocol), 54
Uleman, J., 86
unconscious bias, 115–116
updating your resume, 78–79

V

vendor-specific certification,
  43–44
virtual team, 114
"Voice of SecOps Report
  2022", 112–113
volunteering, 70, 71
VPN (virtual private network),
  27–28
vulnerability assessment, 104

W

We Hack Health podcast, 121
weekly goals, 124
Windows
  attack simulation, 58
  Process Monitor, 50–52
Wireshark, network traffic
  analysis, 52–55
WLB (work-life balance), 119.
  See also time management
  burnout, 121
  diet and exercise, 122
  establishing a baseline,
    122
  mental health, 123
  promotion, 140–142
  sleep, 123
  time management,
    124–125
  tunnel vision, 120

X-Y-Z

YouTube, 75–76

Zuckerberg, M., 129

Register Your Product at informit.com/register

Access additional benefits and save up to 65%* on your next purchase

- Automatically receive a coupon for 35% off books, eBooks, and web editions and 65% off video courses, valid for 30 days. Look for your code in your InformIT cart or the Manage Codes section of your account page.
- Download available product updates.
- Access bonus material if available.**
- Check the box to hear from us and receive exclusive offers on new editions and related products.

InformIT—The Trusted Technology Learning Source

InformIT is the online home of information technology brands at Pearson, the world's leading learning company. At informit.com, you can

- Shop our books, eBooks, and video training. Most eBooks are DRM-Free and include PDF and EPUB files.
- Take advantage of our special offers and promotions (informit.com/promotions).
- Sign up for special offers and content newsletter (informit.com/newsletters).
- Access thousands of free chapters and video lessons.
- Enjoy free ground shipping on U.S. orders.*

* Offers subject to change.
** Registration benefits vary by product. Benefits will be listed on your account page under Registered Products.

Connect with InformIT—Visit informit.com/community

 twitter.com/informit

 Pearson

inform IT

Addison-Wesley • Adobe Press • Cisco Press • Microsoft Press • Oracle Press • Peachpit Press • Pearson IT Certification • Que